What Would Jesus
Deconstruct?

D0165692

THE CHURCH
AND POSTMODERN
CULTURE

James K. A. Smith, series editor
www.churchandpomo.org

The Church and Postmodern
Culture series features high-profile
theorists in continental philosophy
and contemporary theology
writing for a broad, nonspecialist
audience interested in the impact of
postmodern theory on the faith and
practice of the church.

What Would Jesus
Deconstruct?

*The Good News of Postmodernity
for the Church*

John D. Caputo

B
Baker Academic
Grand Rapids, Michigan

© 2007 by John D. Caputo

Published by Baker Academic
a division of Baker Publishing Group
P.O. Box 6287, Grand Rapids, MI 49516–6287
www.bakeracademic.com

Printed in the United States of America

                    Library of Congress Cataloging-in-Publication Data
Caputo, John D.
    What would Jesus deconstruct? : the good news of postmodernity for the church / John D. Caputo.
        p.   cm. — (The church and postmodern culture)
    Includes bibliographical references and index.
    ISBN 10: 0-8010-3136-2 (pbk.)
    ISBN 978-0-8010-3136-6 (pbk.)
    1. Postmodernism—Religious aspects—Christianity. I. Title.
BR115.P74C36 2007
230—dc22   2007019938

Contents

Series Preface

Current discussions in the church—from emergent "postmodern" congregations to mainline "missional" congregations—are increasingly grappling with philosophical and theoretical questions related to postmodernity. In fact, it could be argued that developments in postmodern theory (especially questions of "post-foundationalist" epistemologies) have contributed to the breakdown of former barriers between evangelical, mainline, and Catholic faith communities. Postliberalism—a related "effect" of postmodernism—has engendered a new, confessional ecumenism wherein we find nondenominational evangelical congregations, mainline Protestant churches, and Catholic parishes all wrestling with the challenges of postmodernism and drawing on the culture of postmodernity as an opportunity for rethinking the shape of our churches.

This context presents an exciting opportunity for contemporary philosophy and critical theory to "hit the ground," so to speak, by allowing high-level work in postmodern theory to serve the church's practice—including all the kinds of congregations and communions noted above. The goal of this series is to bring together high-profile theorists in continental philosophy and contemporary theology to write for a broad, nonspecialist audience interested in the impact of postmodern theory on the faith and practice of the church. Each book in the series will, from different angles and with different questions, undertake to answer questions such as What does postmodern theory have to say about the shape of the church? How should concrete, in-the-pew and on-the-ground religious practices be impacted by postmodernism? What should the church look like in postmodernity? What has Paris to do with Jerusalem?

The series is ecumenical not only with respect to its ecclesial destinations but also with respect to the facets of continental philosophy and theory that are represented. A wide variety of theoretical commitments will be included, ranging from deconstruction to Radical Orthodoxy, including voices from Badiou to Žižek and the usual suspects in between (Nietzsche, Heidegger, Levinas, Derrida, Foucault, Irigaray, Rorty, and others). Insofar as postmodernism occasions a retrieval of ancient sources, these contemporary sources will be brought into dialogue with Augustine, Irenaeus, Aquinas, and other resources. Drawing on the wisdom of established scholars in the field, the series will provide accessible introductions to postmodern thought with the specific aim of exploring its impact on ecclesial practice. The books are offered, one might say, as French lessons for the church.

Foreword

Fasten your seatbelts, dear readers, and return your tray tables to their upright and locked positions. You are on the runway and have been cleared for takeoff on a wild flight. Jack Caputo is your pilot. This metaphorical crop duster flies like a clichéd bat out of proverbial hell. His take off will be fast and the winds turbulent, so expect some bumps during your ascent. But rest assured, you're going to love the flight, unless, of course, you are constitutionally predisposed to airsickness, in which case you will find a small white bag with detailed instructions in the seatback in front of you.

I first encountered Jack Caputo's writings in the introduction to *God, the Gift, and Postmodernism*, which he edited with Michael Scanlon (Indiana University Press, 1999). Since I'm not a professional philosopher, a number of the book's chapters (sur)passed the reading comprehension capacities of my bald layman's head, but not the introduction. There Caputo and Scanlon spoke in down-to-earth terms of our need to become "enlightened about the Enlightenment" (meaning, for my fellow less-philosophical laypeople, the eighteenth-century movement that eventually reduced reality to phenomena that could be measured and dissected by "objective" human reason). They explained,

> We sought to seize the contemporary moment which has loosened the grip of the old Enlightenment, questioned its intimidating authority, complained about the exclusionary force of its certainties and axioms (among which secularism has enjoyed pride of

place), and thereby made some room for a religious discourse and restored the voice of a religious imagination, the Enlightenment . . . having chased away one ghost too many. Our wager was, the more enlightened we get about the Enlightenment, the more likely religion is to get a word in edgewise. (pp. 1–2)

As a pastor (and beginning writer) grappling with the whole swarm of issues that nests in the eaves of the term "postmodern," I was lured by those few sentences to become a fan of Jack's work. I'm still hooked.

Since that first exposure, I have read several more books by Jack, including *Philosophy and Theology* (2006), *Prayers and Tears of Jacques Derrida* (1997), and *Deconstruction in a Nutshell* (1996). I also had the chance to hear him speak in public on several occasions. In both written and live venues, Caputo struck me as the most comprehensible philosopher I had come across—and not just clear, but also downright entertaining. I have never heard him give a lecture that didn't make me laugh out loud, and, of course, we all know that learning sneaks up on us best when we're distracted by laughter. Remember, we're talking about a philosopher here. (The line between the best philosophers and the best comedians may not be as thick as we think.)

My wife heard me chuckling audibly while reading the book you're now holding, which, in addition to being (a) comprehensible to normal PWD humans,[1] (b) substantially philosophical, and (c) profoundly religious in theme, is also (d) sparklingly written and (e) downright fun. It is also (f) serious and (g) passionate, and, I think, (h) substantially true, or at least inspirationally capable of motivating its readers to *make true* things that *should be* true.

Overly long forewords soak up time that would be better spent reading the actual book, so before signing off I'll briefly act as a flight attendant might, telling you a couple of things you should look out for during your flight—you know, "The Grand Canyon is visible to those sitting in the A seats now," or "If you're in the F seats, you can get a great view of the St. Louis Arch coming up on our right."

First, you'll notice that Jack flies you into a "zone of intertextuality," meaning that he is going to suspend you between several texts, notably Sheldon's *In His Steps* (the unlikely inspiration of the WWJD craze), the writings of Jacques Derrida, and the New

Testament. This may strike you as an unlikely combination, but it will make perfect sense by the time you're halfway to the last page.

Second, you'll notice that Jack is (like many of us) haunted by the fading but powerful ghost of the Religious Right, which hovers ominously over his right (of course) shoulder throughout the book. He keeps speaking to the ghost in parentheses, which is very hospitable of him, a kind of "making room for the other," if you will. If you are yourself affiliated with this ghost, be sure to take advantage of this hospitality.

Third, don't miss Jack's penchant for poignant, unexpected, startlingly insightful definitions, often delivered grammatically in the appositive position, meaning directly after the word they're defining, as in this sentence. In particular, keep your eyes open for his definitions of *heresy*, *the real*, *hospitality*, *the gift*, or *the legal*, and, of course, the ever-popular and always-(mis)understood *deconstruction*.

Finally, perk up whenever Jack uses the term *journey* or any term related to it, such as *steps*, *adventure*, *lost*, *way*, and so on. Even though Jack poses as a scholar without pastoral credentials or instincts, this pose must be deconstructed in light of Jack's not-very-well camouflaged pastoral desire to actually edify or encourage his readers to notice, consider, and maybe even seek to follow the way of Jesus—deconstructing what Jesus deconstructed, for starters. Like deconstruction itself, these chapters can rightly be taken as expressions or outbursts of love, which means that as a willing reader, you are making yourself susceptible to the possibility of being edified, encouraged, and (gulp) loved.

As you can tell, I really enjoyed this book, every chapter. It stirred up afresh in me the love of wisdom that is what philosophy is supposed to be about. At a deeper level, it fanned the embers of desire for (to quote Jack) "what we love and pray for," namely, "that which withdraws, that which is already withdrawn and whose approach is always coming, always already coming, that which is never present but always drawing us out by withdrawing itself, soliciting and inviting us, luring us"—in other words, the unnamable, hypernymous (don't worry about that word, Jack never uses it) event that is called or invited to show up and interrupt when we say the word "God," a word that, unlike the reality of which it is a faint trace, can be deconstructed.

OK, now I'm just soaking up valuable time. It's time to let Jack take you up for a test flight of some wonderful ideas and dreams. The safety demonstration is over. Turn off those portable electronic devices.

Brian McLaren
Laurel, Maryland
Brianmclaren.net

Acknowledgments

My thanks to Sharon Baker (Messiah College), B. Keith Putt (Samford University) and Elizabeth Morgan (Eastern University), who have read this manuscript for me and have been a constant source of good advice. My special thanks to Jamie Smith and Robert Hosack for having invited me to contribute to this book series and to Jamie in particular for his encouragement throughout and for an extremely thorough reading of the manuscript at a critical point in its composition. The whole idea may be blamed on Brian McLaren whose invitation to speak at an Emergent Youth Specialties Convention in 2004 resulted in a presentation entitled "Why the Church Deserves Deconstruction," which spawned the present work. A few pages of this book, indicated in the endnotes, are excerpted from "Theopoetic/Theopolitic" (with Catherine Keller), *Cross-Currents* 56, no. 4 (Winter 2007): 105–11, and "Beyond Sovereignty: Many Nations under the Weakness of God," *Soundings: An Interdisciplinary Journal* 89, nos. 1–2 (Spring-Summer 2006): 21–35.

Introduction

JAMES K. A. SMITH

The *Church and Postmodern Culture* series is a "big tent" venture. Both continental philosophy and on-the-ground religious movements are prone to the formulation of party lines—with all the attendant shibboleths. The result is a rather tribal isolation; each party carves out its own spaces for discussion and dialogue, but most of this turns out to be preaching to the choir. Or, to run with the opening metaphor, what we get is a proliferation of tents. The shape of the *Church and Postmodern Culture* series is intended to counter such party-think and the ensuing withdrawal into smaller and smaller tents. Instead we are looking to raise a big tent with rather porous, flapping walls (critics will be glad for an excuse to talk about our three-ring circus)—a big tent that can absorb a number of different troupes all grappling with the central issues facing the church in postmodernity.

It is my hope that this "big tent" sensibility can already be sensed in our opening volumes. Whereas my *Who's Afraid of Postmodernism?* ended with a call for a more radical orthodoxy and the suggestion that postmoderns could do no better than be Catholic, John Caputo's *What Would Jesus Deconstruct?* winsomely articulates why so many people are nervous about orthodoxy—radical or not—and suggests that Catholics need to think more seriously about being postmodern. That both of these visions can put on a show in the same tent is, I think, an

indication of the sort of pluralism that is meant to animate the
series. It is, I hope, a big tent with no center ring, just a spotlight
that shifts from book to book.

What Would Jesus Deconstruct? shifts the spotlight to a per-
former who, oddly, doesn't often get center stage in these discussions: Jesus. While the reader might be tempted to assume that
Jacques Derrida is the star of this performance, in fact Derrida
here plays the role of the art critic—a commentator who gives us
a lens and a lexicon to see the phenomena in a new light.

Indeed, it was Derrida who emphasized that deconstruction
isn't something that we *do* to things; deconstruction *happens*. And
it happens in the middle voice. So if Caputo sketches a certain
deconstruction of the church, this isn't because he has brought the
Derrida hammer down on this venerable institution. The church
doesn't need Jacques Derrida in order to be deconstructed, because
it's got Jesus! The deconstruction of the church happens from the
inside. And the burden of Caputo's book is to show us that that's a
good thing. Deconstruction is a work of love, and deconstruction
happens because it is animated by a vision for something different. Just as the law is deconstructed with a view to the advent of
justice, so the church is deconstructed with a view to the advent
of the kingdom.

Thus Caputo here plays the role of witness and midwife, giving
voice to the ways in which Jesus's vision of the kingdom decon-
structs all our domestications—not to leave the institution razed
to the ground, but merely flattened. In fact, the whole project is
animated by a passion for just institutions—a desire to see things
otherwise, to see an institution opened to the Other, to the future,
and most importantly, to a Jesus who will surprise us. One might
say that Caputo envisages a "charismatic" institution—the sort of
thing that can only sound like an oxymoron to the modernism of
Max Weber and his ilk.

The critique of the domesticated Jesus has a long pedigree,
perhaps the most notable being Dostoyevsky's chilling account
of Jesus having the audacity to show up and disturb the machi-
nations of the crusades in Seville (which, in fact, Jesus doesn't
disturb at all precisely because his nonviolence can be so easily
silenced). It is a prophetic trope that one can even find *before* Jesus,
in voices like Amos and Jeremiah, who railed against all the ways
Yahweh had been enlisted to legitimate the status quo. Since all

our domestications of Jesus are inevitably local, it should be no surprise that Caputo's critique is directed most specifically against the distinctly American domestication of Jesus associated today with "the Religious Right." Those who have come to see Jesus as Superman—defender of freedom, justice, and the American way—will bristle at this. That will be a sure sign that Caputo's argument is working. Those who want to remain comfortable will try to convince themselves that they misread the title: that the book is really asking, *What Would Caputo Deconstruct?* Or *What Would Derrida Deconstruct?*

But that's not the question Caputo is asking. His vocation is to be first and foremost a conduit and witness: he wants nothing less than to confront us with a Jesus who resists all our domestications. In and through humor that will have you laughing out loud, Caputo is dead serious. Here is a book in the tradition of John the Baptist, out to make way for a Messiah who, when he shows up, will ruin all our parties. And so Caputo invites us to ask: What would happen if Jesus showed up in Colorado Springs? Or slowly made his way down the aisle on "Justice Sunday" in Kansas? What would Jesus deconstruct if he was sitting across from Al Moehler on *Larry King Live*? What would Jesus deconstruct if he made an appearance at the denominational offices of the Southern Baptist Convention, or, on the other end, the Episcopal Church in the USA? And for that matter, what would Jesus deconstruct if he showed up at our comfy coffee-house "congregations" while we listen to jazz vespers? It is a sign of the vitality of the book that Caputo leaves us with a question that's still alive when we finish: it is a haunting, prophetic question. And he convinces us that we will best serve Jesus's coming kingdom by never ceasing to ask the question.

1

In His Steps—
A Postmodern Edition

In 1896, Charles Sheldon, a pastor in Topeka, Kansas, wrote a book titled *In His Steps*.[1] The subtitle of Sheldon's book, *What Would Jesus Do?* fueled the later "WWJD" industry—the bumper stickers, T-shirts, and bracelets that boldly pose a question to which the Religious Right is sure it knows the answer. My hypothesis is if our friends on the Right really mean to *ask* that question instead of using it as a stick to beat their enemies, they are in for a shock. The book has gone through numerous editions and there are estimates—no one knows for sure—that it has sold some 30 million copies, putting it right up there with the Bible. If so, it will perhaps do no harm if I propose a new edition, let us say a Postmodern Collector's Edition, a special two-disk DVD set that will contain Sheldon's text on one disk and numerous bonus features that will include a postmodern running commentary on the other. Imagine Jacques Derrida running in the steps of Charles Sheldon, or maybe just out there jogging alongside him down some country road in turn-of-the-century Topeka. That is a bizarre image, unforgivable really, and I beg the forgiveness of everyone concerned: of those who love the question "What Would Jesus Do?"—I love it too, although I am also afraid of it and think it is a very tricky two-edged sword—

and of my deconstructionist friends, who are appalled to see me associate deconstruction with the politics of rural Kansas and a question that has been condensed to bumper-sticker simplicity.[2] What gives me the courage to go on is that in both Jesus and deconstruction forgiveness enjoys pride of place and that the most perfect form of forgiveness is to forgive unforgivable offenses, like the one I here propose to commit. I pin everything on the hope that we have all done something we are ashamed of and no one will have the courage to cast the first stone.

What Would Jesus Do?

Sheldon hit on the idea of holding his congregation's attention by way of a series of weekly sermons that would in fact be a serialized novel, with cliff-hanger endings each week that would draw the congregation back on the following Sunday, an idea that the creators of TV series like *24* have since seized on with great success. In the opening chapter—it was published a year later as a book—a homeless man, in his early thirties (the traditional age of Jesus at his death), disturbs the decorum of the Sunday morning services of the First Church of Raymond, the most proper and prosperous church in town. Were I to produce a film version of the book I would look for someone like the Henry Fonda of *Grapes of Wrath* to play this character, someone soft spoken but whose words rise up from the depths. The choir has given a particularly excellent rendition of "Jesus, I my cross have taken, All to leave and follow Thee." The pastor, Rev. Henry Maxwell, has just concluded a stirring sermon on 1 Peter 2:21: "For hereunto were ye called; because Christ also suffered for you, leaving you an example that ye should follow his steps" (I have retained language of the King James Version used in the novel for a reason). Then, at just that precise moment, the bedraggled young man comes forward and addresses a startled congregation:

> "I'm not an ordinary tramp, though I don't know of any teaching of Jesus that makes one kind of a tramp less worth saving than another. Do you?" He put the question as naturally as if the whole congregation had been a small Bible class. He paused just a moment and coughed painfully. Then he went on. (*In His Steps*, 8)

He recounts a Dickensesque story of misfortune. He has lost his job as a typesetter, his wife died in a desperate New York City tenement (owned by Christians), and he can no longer care for his daughter, who now lives with a friend. After reporting his futile attempts to find help in their community despite three days of trying, he concludes:

> It seems to me there's an awful lot of trouble in the world that somehow wouldn't exist if all the people who sing such songs went and lived them out. I suppose I don't understand. But what would Jesus do? (*In His Steps*, 10)

Then he gives a "queer lurch" and falls in a heap on the church floor. A doctor rushes to his side and reports, "He seems to have a heart problem." That is as close to a double entendre as you will find in Sheldon, for whatever physical ailments the man's poverty has caused, he certainly has a broken heart! Is he dead or alive? Will he recover? The picture fades. Come back next week if you want to find out.

The following Sunday the faithful in Topeka packed the church to learn that the man had later died in the home of Rev. Maxwell. That proves to be a week of fateful soul searching for the pastor, who finds himself face-to-face with the man's dying words, which he in turn puts to Raymond's best: Are you ready to take the pledge? To do what Jesus would do? A shudder is sent through the powers that be in town—the local college president; the editor of the town newspaper; the superintendent of railroads; and one Virginia Page, an heiress who had just inherited a million dollars, "a statuesque blonde of attractive proportions," which is evidently how such matters were put in 1896 Topeka (we have since come up with other language). The novel goes on to tell the story of the transformation that takes place in the lives of everyone.

Thus was born the question "What would Jesus do?" Because Sheldon failed to secure a proper copyright, the book was allowed to gain a wide circulation. Sheldon distributed what royalties he did receive among his numerous charitable causes. *In His Steps* is not going to make it on most "Great Books" lists. It is sentimental and a bit simplistic; it is preachy and a bit pietistic; its characters are thinly disguised props for ideas; and the King James version of the Bible it uses is a good fit for its stilted and theatrical style.

Still, it would be excessively snooty for an academic like myself to dwell on its literary limitations, which is basically to congratulate myself for not having written a book that has sold 30 million copies. The book has a certain charm and a few dramatic twists that probably passed for cliff-hangers in Kansas, and it has managed to communicate something of permanent and central importance about the gospel, about its prophetic message of generosity toward the most dispossessed and disadvantaged, and about the serious social obligations of Christians. It got this message out to large numbers of Christians, well beyond the numbers reached by much weightier tomes of theology or scholarly articles in the *Journal of the American Academy of Religion*.

I commend the reading of this book to Christians, left, right, and center, not all of whom may realize today where this famous question comes from. It will be an eye opener to the Christian Right, who, having tried to blackmail us with this question, will discover that the slogan they have been wearing on their T-shirts and pasting on their automobile bumpers all these years is a call for radical social justice! That may precipitate a spate of garage sales all over suburban Christendom, where well-scrubbed Bible thumpers will seek to rid themselves of such subversive paraphernalia or, at the very least, to keep them away from the children. (The Left, by contrast, would stand to pick up some bargains were it not so terrified of religion.) So even if, as I concede, Charles Sheldon is no Charles Dickens—or Reinhold Niebuhr or Dietrich Bonhoeffer, for that matter—he is the author of a question that has captured the minds and hearts of millions of Americans today, and he is worth another look.[3]

Trained at Phillips Academy, Brown University, and Andover Theological Seminary, Sheldon was a formative influence on the Social Gospel movement, and he put the gospel personally into practice. He spent periods of time living among the poor and working class of Topeka, including time in "Tennesseetown" (the "Rectangle" in Raymond)—a large black ghetto not far from his church—to which he dedicated considerable attention. He was a critic of racism in the church and of the Ku Klux Klan in particular, and he advocated equality for women in the church—they figure prominently in *In His Steps*—and in society at large.

Sheldon called for personal transformation and personal responsibility, which was his evangelical side, but at the same time he was attentive to the larger issue of the need for social and structural transformation, which was his Christian-socialist side. His focus on alcoholism is typical. He thought alcoholism was in part a matter of character and willpower, which is certainly true, but he also understood that it was a social problem and very much a function of systemic poverty and unbridled capitalism. As the statuesque Virginia Page says, "The saloon furnishes material to be saved faster than the settlement or residence or rescue mission work can save it" (*In His Steps*, 127). Or as Jim Wallis, one of the leading figures in the current movement for a progressive evangelical Christianity, likes to say, it's not enough to keep pulling bodies from the river; we must go upstream to see who is throwing them in. Not only do hearts have to be changed, but the system has to be fixed. Sheldon's solution—Prohibition—was ill conceived—the Irish would never go for it—but one can see what he was thinking about. Alcoholism was the drug scene of his day, before the days of hard drugs and the massive violence on the streets that accompanies it, and it required something more radical and more thoughtful than telling people to just say no, which is easy to say and, besides, allows us to keep our money in our pocket. Sheldon was also a great advocate of Sabbatarianism, which is also very evangelical and offensive to the modern secular lifestyle. But Sheldon viewed this issue in terms of an unfettered capitalism that, already benefiting from a twelve-hour workday in the days before effective labor laws, wanted a seven-day work week. The Christianity of *In His Steps* is an interesting mix of the personal and the structural, of generosity of spirit accompanied by social consciousness and a prophetic politics. Sheldon wanted to bring the kingdom of God to earth, or at least get a running start on it by following in Jesus's steps.

John Howard Yoder criticizes Sheldon's Jesus for being a kind of blanket moral template, a universal moral paradigm, which just stands for anything good—like a walking, talking categorical imperative—and not paying attention to details. By this Yoder means pacifism.[4] Philosophers reading this book—I am assuming a lot here—might be led to wonder how much mileage can be gotten out of asking a substitute question like "What would Socrates do?" Take the case of Alexander Powers, superintendent of the local railroad in *In His Steps*, who took measures to improve the working conditions of the railroad employees but who resigned after blowing the whistle on the company when he discovered it was in violation of interstate commerce laws. Superintendent Powers could easily have gotten that far with Socrates, who taught that the good of the soul is virtue and that the only true evil is the evil that we do, not the evil that is done to us for doing good. In fact, there is a precedent for Sheldon's question in the philosopher Epictetus, who asked what Socrates or Zeno would do.[5] So one central problem among the many problems posed by this question is to determine what is the *specifically* Jesus-like thing that we are called to do.

Sheldon's novel influenced theologian Walter Rauschenbusch, one of the founding fathers of a theology of the Social Gospel. This theology brought the teachings of Jesus to bear on problems of social justice, like poverty, public health, underfunded schools, child labor, slums, the conditions of immigrants, and war and peace. The Social Gospel theology flourished in the first half of the century and was prominent throughout the New Deal days. Later, its prophetic spirit could be felt in the work of Martin Luther King Jr. and liberation theology. Today it is present in movements like Jim Wallis's "Sojourners/Call to Renewal."[6] Sheldon's own popularity fell on hard times with the collapse of Prohibition, which made for an ironic end given that one of the things Jesus did do was drink wine—in moderation! Jesus did not use the wine shortage at Cana to announce the new law of Prohibition but to make more wine for the party (not to mention Socrates, who was famous for being able to drink all night and still keep his argument straight). Sheldon thought that if there were "saloons" in Galilee, Jesus would have spoken out against them.

I refer to that only half in jest because it raises a problem that goes to the heart of asking, "What would Jesus do?" It is too easy to use this question to spiritually intimidate our enemies, which is why the question is so frightening. The question should be turned first to ourselves so as to put ourselves in question—"in the accusative," as Levinas would say—instead of being used as a beam, as in a two-by-four, to slam others. The question is tricky, not a magic bullet, because everybody left or right wants Jesus on their side (instead of the other way around). It requires an immense amount of interpretation, interpolation, and self-questioning to give it any bite—and if it is not biting *us*, it has no bite—lest it be just a way of getting others to do what I want them to do but under the cover of Jesus. The "would" in the question carries all this weight; it is the bump in the road of following in his steps. The "would" draws us into what contemporary philosophers call "hermeneutics," the theory of interpretation. How big a bump "hermeneutics" is can be gleaned from Nietzsche, who said "there are no facts, only interpretations" (and quoting Nietzsche is the best way I know to clear a room of evangelical Christians). So another question posed by the question "What would Jesus do?" is how much work can it actually get done once we appreciate its complexity. It does not make things easier, only harder. That is why I here call on the aid of deconstruction—another evangelical room clearer—which I sometimes camouflage as "radical hermeneutics," to help us out.

Adding a Dash of Deconstruction

Consider the fate of Sheldon's question. The heroes of Sheldon's novel renounce the profit-making motives that drive capitalism and give up luxury and success for the sake of living among and working on behalf of the poorest of the poor. They are evangelical counterparts to people like Dorothy Day, Mother Teresa, Martin Luther King Jr., and Archbishop Desmond Tutu. The ever-growing extremes of rich and poor in today's globalized capitalism remind us of the "Gilded Age," the world of the Carnegies and other moguls of unregulated capitalism, in Sheldon's world. But the original force of Sheldon's question has been turned upside down in the barrage of bracelets and televangelists preaching personal wealth as a sign of God's approval.

With that in mind, let us revisit Sheldon's opening scene, the lovely Sunday morning, a gathering of "the best dressed, most comfortable-looking people in Raymond," the beautiful choir, the eloquent pastor:

> Suddenly, into the midst of this perfect accord and concord between preacher and audience, there came a very remarkable interruption. It would be difficult to indicate the extent of the shock which this interruption measured. It was so unexpected, so entirely contrary to any thought of any person present that it offered no room for argument or, for the time being, of resistance. (*In His Steps*, 6)

An incongruous and unsettling figure, uncomely and uncanny, disturbs the Sunday serenity. Hitherto comfortable lives are turned upside down. Jobs are lost, careers are abandoned, fortunes given away, businesses go under, divisions are introduced among friends and families, parents are turned against children; harmony becomes cacophony. What would Jesus do—if he ever showed up some Sunday morning? Turn things upside down. The last would be first, the meek and poor would inherit the earth, the hungry would be given good things, and the rich would be sent away empty (Luke 1:53). Do you think he would bring peace? No, not peace, but the sword. Would he preach "family values"? No, he advocates hating father and mother for the kingdom of God. Instead of being confirmed in our ways and congratulated on our virtue, we would stand accused, looking for the log in our own eye rather than the sliver in the eye of the other. "Jesus is a great divider of life," Sheldon says (*In His Steps*, 113).

To put Sheldon's point in other words, we who are sometimes known to use the ungodly idiom of contemporary French theory might say: into the sphere of the "same" (the familiar, the customary, the business-as-usual of Sunday services) bursts the "advent" or the "event" of the "other," of the "coming of the other," which makes the same tremble and reconfigure. In these other words, Sheldon's strategy is to open the novel with a scene of *deconstruction* (whose honor, like Mary Magdalene's, I hope to see restored!). In Sheldon's story the homeless man's identity (Jack Manning) is revealed in the next chapter. I could imagine, in the manner of the supernaturalist films of our day, like *The Sixth Sense*, leaving him nameless, an unknown and mysterious placeholder, thereby suggesting a miraculous appearance of Jesus himself come to the town of Raymond for a new holy week, during which he suffered and died again. What I will analyze as the "event"—what's really happening there—that stirs within the figure of Jesus is that of a deep deconstructive force or agency. Mark C. Taylor once famously described deconstruction as the hermeneutics of the death of God.[7] But in the view I am advancing here, deconstruction is treated as the hermeneutics of the *kingdom* of God, as an interpretive style that helps get at the prophetic spirit of Jesus—who was a surprising and sometime strident outsider, who took a stand with the "other"—and thereby helps us get a fix on Sheldon's sometimes slippery question. In my view, a deconstruction is good news, because it delivers the shock of the other to the forces of the same, the shock of the good (the "ought") to the forces of being ("what is"), which is also why I think it bears good news to the church.

Contrary to what you may have read in some Christian presses, the "other" is not the devil himself but a figure of the *truth*, a truth that has been safely closeted away or repressed. Notice that Sheldon's unnerving "tramp"—one of Derrida's last books was titled *Rogues*—this figure of the "other," does not rant and rave: "There was nothing offensive in the man's manner or tone. He was not excited, and he spoke in a low but distinct voice" (*In His Steps*, 7).

He speaks simply, quietly, but the impact of his words is lost on no one. Things get deconstructed by the *event of truth* that they harbor, an event that sets off unforeseeable and disruptive consequences:

> Gradually the truth was growing upon him that the pledge to do as Jesus would was working out a revolution in his parish and through-out the city. Every day added to the serious results of obedience to that pledge. Maxwell did not pretend to see the end. He was, in fact, only now at the very beginning of events that were destined to change the history of hundreds of families not only in Raymond but throughout the entire country. (*In His Steps*, 72)

So the "event" need not be delivered by a thunderbolt. It gradually, quietly overtakes us, grows on us, until at a certain point we realize that everything has been transformed. In a deconstruction, our lives, our beliefs, and our practices are not destroyed but forced to reform and reconfigure—which is risky business. In the New Testament this is called *metanoia*, or undergoing a fundamental change of heart. Our hearts are turned inside out not by a vandal but by an angel or evangel of the *truth*, the truth that we say we embrace but that now, up close, looks ominous, frightening, ugly, and even smells bad. What if the truth smells bad? What if the poor, who are blessed in the kingdom, do not have the opportunity to bathe regularly? We sing songs to the truth as if it were a source of comfort, warmth, and good hygiene. But in deconstruction the truth is dangerous, and it will drive you out into the cold. Nietzsche had it right when he said we lack the courage for the truth, that the truth will make us stronger just so long as it doesn't kill us first.

We want the truth attenuated, softened, bathed, and powdered, like the smarmy depictions of Jesus looking up to heaven found on the covers of some editions of *In His Steps*.

These editors would do better to put the ghettos of the "Rectangle" on the cover, because Sheldon's point was that Jesus is most likely to be found in the worst slums, among the most dispossessed people, on the most dangerous streets in a modern city. My own proposal for the cover of my postmodern edition of *In His Steps* is to use a scene from the HBO series *The Wire*. The best contemporary counterpart to the "Rectangle"—Sheldon's idea of the people Jesus had in mind when he announced his mission, "The Spirit of the Lord is upon me, because he has anointed me to bring good news to the poor" (Luke 4:18)—is the drug scene in the inner-city ghettos like those in Baltimore, whose grim violence is unforgettably etched in our mind by the stunning cinematography of *The Wire*. In the midst of the mindlessness of much commercial television, there are artists willing to speak the truth, in this case to honestly portray what I consider the very world that Jesus said constituted his mission. *The Wire* is as complicated to follow as a Russian novel—which reflects the complexity of moral life itself—and, like Dostoyevsky, is as high minded and as tragic about the drama of good and evil. If you want to see what Sheldon's Jesus would do, to see someone Christlike translated into the terms of the twenty-first century, someone walking in the steps of Jesus, then study the people who are trying to intervene in that world. Someone like "Prez," the teacher, gentle as a lamb in the midst of wolves, who spends himself on behalf of the children in his class. Prez's work is blocked not only by the merciless poverty and violence of the world in which his students live but also by academic programs devised by demagogues, which compel teachers to stop teaching and "teach the test," to stop addressing the singular needs of children in singular situations and teach a standardized test. Or "McNulty" and "Bunny Colvin," policemen as self-conflicted as St. Paul, who understand perfectly that the powers that be, the "(City) Hall," are people who are interested not in alleviating misery and reducing crime on the street but in accumulating favorable but meaningless statistics that will ensure their reelection. Or the children on the street, like "Dee" or "Randy," who tried in vain to lift themselves out of a world saturated with crime. *The Wire* is a postmodern parable set not in the olive groves of ancient Galilee but in the streets of the contemporary inner city. There everything Jesus meant by the kingdom, and everything Paul meant by grace and the new being, fights a losing battle with the powers of this world and with the whitened sepulchers whose fathers killed the prophets.[8]

The Wire gives us an idea of how a deconstruction works. It simply tells the truth, meticulously, uncompromisingly, without disguise, amelioration, or artificial sweeteners. In a deconstruction, things are made to tremble by their own inner impulse, by a force that will give them no rest, that keeps forcing itself to the surface, forcing itself out, making the thing restless. Deconstruction is organized around the idea that things contain a kind of uncontainable truth, that they contain what they cannot contain. Nobody has to come along and "deconstruct" things. Things are auto-deconstructed by the tendencies of their own inner truth. In a deconstruction, the "other" is the one who tells the truth on the "same"; the other is the truth of the same, the truth that has been repressed and suppressed, omitted and marginalized, or sometimes just plain murdered, like Jesus himself, which is why Johannes Baptist Metz speaks of the "dangerous memory" of the suffering of Jesus[9] and why I describe deconstruction as a hermeneutics of the kingdom of God.[10]

The "danger" Metz describes is the deconstructive force. As soon as the "other" tells the truth, as soon as the truth is out, then the beliefs or the practices, the texts or institutions, that have been entrusted with that truth begin to tremble! Then they have to reconfigure, reorganize, regroup, reassemble in order to come to grips with their inner tendencies—or repress them all the more mightily. So Sheldon is effectively proposing a "deconstruction of the church," a deconstruction of what calls itself Christianity, "a challenge to Christianity as it is practiced in our churches" (*In His Steps*, 14). The assembly (*ecclesia*) of the First Church of Raymond, Kansas, is called to *re*-assemble, to regroup, called to a new order, by a shocking Christlike street person who comes bearing the truth. If the truth can make us free, as we all so readily agree, it cannot do so without a deconstruction, which is a way of making, or letting, the truth happen. The truth is not the stuff of edifying hymns, rather it is dangerous, dirty, and smelly business. To seek the truth is to play with fire and a way to get burned. Not everyone has a stomach for it, above all those who say "Lord, Lord" and then head for cover the minute the Lord shows up dressed in rags and smelling like a street person. Be careful what you pray for. Lord, give me the truth—but not yet! The next time we look up to heaven and piously pray "Come, Lord Jesus," we may find that he is already here, trying to get warm over an urban steam grate or trying to cross our borders.

On my reading, which will sound a little too pious to impious deconstructors and downright impious to good and pious Christians, deconstruction is a theory of *truth*, in which truth spells *trouble*. As does Jesus. That is what they have in common. The truth will make you free, but it does so by turning your life upside down. Up to now, deconstruction has gotten a lot of mileage out of taking sides with the *"un-*truth." That is a methodological irony, a strategy of "reversal," meant to expose the contingency of what we like to call the "Truth," with a capital T—deconstruction being a critique of long-robed totalizers of a capitalized Truth, of T-totallers of all kinds. I have no intention of sending that strategy into early retirement or claiming that it has outlived its usefulness. We will need that strategy as long as there is hypocrisy, as long as there are demagogues pounding on the table that they have the Truth, which means forever. Indeed, I will not hesitate to make use of that strategy here. But I do want to supplement it with a complementary theory of truth. For while deconstructors have made important gains exposing the hypocrisy of temporal and contingent claims that portray themselves in the long robes of Eternal Verity, it is also necessary to point out that deconstruction is at the same time a hermeneutics of truth, of the truth of the event, which is not deconstructible. This is the truth that disturbs and that we tend to repress. When a deconstruction is done well, the truth or—what seems like the same thing—all hell will break out. What the truth does, what this Christlike figure in Sheldon's novel does, or their contemporary counterparts in *The Wire* do, what Jesus does, is deconstruct. Sheldon's famous novel, this classic of popular Christian piety, the one with the smarmy picture of Jesus on the cover, turns on a—hold your ears—*deconstruction*. Jesus Christ, Deconstructor![11]

Imagine the scene: a miraculous reappearance of another Christlike tramp, of Jesus himself incognito, at Sunday morning services in the churches of America. Jesus as an illegal migrant worker, a "wetback" who can barely speak English, or a street person with dirty hands and grubby clothes intruding on the well-scrubbed, smartly garbed congregations of suburban Christendom, which is doing everything to keep him out.

So there is a kick in this bumper-sticker question that the Christian Right did not anticipate. It was posed by a man who looked kindly on the idea of a Christian socialism and pointed with admiration to the communal lives of the early Christians. It contains a truth that will take by surprise those who wear it proudly on their T-shirts, those who repeat this question without quite knowing its history, who may just find themselves auto-deconstructed. What would Jesus do? He would deconstruct a very great deal of what people do in the name of Jesus, starting with the people who wield this question like a hammer to beat their enemies. My hypothesis is that the first thing that Jesus would deconstruct is WWJD itself, the whole "industry," the whole commercial operation of spiritual and very real money-making Christian capitalists.

The Church Is Plan B

Sheldon is evoking an old and venerable scene, one that—rightly—haunts the Christian imagination. We are always, constantly, structurally haunted by the memory of Jesus, by the unnerving prospect that one day Jesus will drop by, unannounced. I do not mean in the decisive day of the second coming but on an ordinary day, some Sunday morning say, as in Sheldon's scenario, simply to pay us an interim visit, to look in on what is going on in his name. Sheldon restages in 1896 Topeka the scene that Dostoyevsky staged in the famous "Legend of the Grand Inquisitor" in sixteenth-century Seville. Jesus appears one day among the common people outside the cathedral in Seville, once again making the blind see and the dead rise. The ancient cardinal, who recognizes that this mysterious figure is indeed Jesus, has him summarily arrested—with but the least movement of his little finger, "such is his power." Paying Jesus a visit in his cell that night, the cardinal asks him why he came back to earth. The work of Jesus is over and now the power has been passed to the pope. His return can represent only an interference. For this reason, the cardinal sentences Jesus to be burned at the stake the next morning, just as he has burned hundreds of heretics the day before—a "heretic" meaning anyone who interferes with the work of the church, including Jesus.

While I do not think this is a perfect story as to its details, its larger point stands.[12] The church tends by the inner momentum of its institutional structure to assert its own authority, to authorize itself. The church behaves exactly as if it itself has fed the Jesus of the New Testament the line, "Thou art Peter and on this Rock I will build my church," which, by the way, is actually what the historical-critical New Testament scholars argue. The church authorizes or founds itself by invoking the authority of a Founder who did not intend to found anything but to announce the good news that the kingdom of God was at hand and the end time was in sight. The church acts exactly as if it is self-authorizing, so that its work can only be interrupted and endangered were anyone to interfere, including Jesus himself, if he returned to see what is going on in his name. The church is not about to have its power questioned and its dogmas thrown into confusion by letting anything of that sort transpire. Having gotten used to the idea that the church defines and determines what Jesus stands for, and what Jesus would do, the church is not going to see its authority threatened by anyone, not even by Jesus himself. Whoever defies the teachings of the church by definition stands accused of heresy— and that goes for Jesus. In short, were Jesus to return in the flesh, he would be executed again, not by the world but by the church. Or left by the church to die in the cold, like Sheldon's character, or to be shot down in the nightmare violence of America's urban warfare because Christians support right-wing extremists opposed to gun control, or excluded as an illegal immigrant.

The fundamental fact about the church is the structural gap, the irreducible distance, that exists between itself and Jesus, a gap expressed by the fateful subjunctive, the "would" in "What would Jesus do?" of which it needs to remind itself first, last, and always, and the concomitant shock that would be delivered to itself—not to mention the shock that would be delivered to Jesus—were Jesus himself ever to set foot in one of its churches. In that gap there lies embedded the principle of a deconstruction of Christianity, in which a deconstruction would effect not a destruction but a reconfiguration aroused by reviving the memory of Jesus. Deconstruction is memory. What would Jesus do—if he ever saw what you and I are doing in his name? Weep, as he wept over Jerusalem. What would Christians do? Head for the doors. The opening scene of Sheldon's novel gets it exactly right. Jesus would be just the sort of unnerving, scary, smelly, and marginal character who would clear the room, the sort that would cause a lot of Christians to cross to the other side of the street if they saw him approaching, the kind of fellow who sends "For Sale" signs springing up all over suburban Christendom for fear the neighborhood is going and property values will decline. For his part, Jesus would be mystified by what is going on, which would seem to him the very thing he targeted in his preaching and parables.

By asking what Jesus would *deconstruct* I am trying to be provocative, but I am also, as always, in earnest about this word "deconstruction." I value it on several levels. It is an exemplary case of avant-garde French "theory" that throws a scare into the elect, and on this point the title of James K. A. Smith's *Who's Afraid of Postmodernism?* strikes the right note.[13] Furthermore, and this is a line I have been peddling for a while, in virtue of its deeply biblical resonances, deconstruction provides a felicitous hermeneutic of the kingdom of God, or so I hope to show.[14] It announces the good news about alterity, which it bears to the church. It has prophetic resonances that call for justice to flow like water over the land. So I am employing the word in a rigorous sense here, not trying to stretch it just to produce a shock or pander to a biblical audience. I am proposing that what happens in deconstruction has an inner sympathy with the very "kingdom of God" that Jesus calls for—which suggests the need for a companion book by a French theorist addressed to secular deconstructors titled *Who's Afraid of the New Testament?* (That is the sort of thing Slavoj Žižek has been doing in his own way.)

Posed in the subjunctive, what *would* Jesus do or deconstruct, the question turns on the structure of the archive, of memory and repetition. How does the New Testament preserve the memory of Jesus? I prescind from all historical-critical questions here, which open up another abyss (about the *arche* itself). One abyss at a time! I treat the New Testament as an "archive," a depository of memories, which presents a certain way to be, a certain "poetics"—not a politics or an ethics or a church dogmatics—that I like to call a "poetics of the kingdom," which lays claim to us and which calls for a "transformation into existence."[15] How are we to translate this soaring poetics into reality? Were this figure of Jesus, who is the

centerpiece of this poetics or theo-poetics, to return today, what
would he look like? An illegal immigrant? A child dying of AIDS?
A Vatican bureaucrat? And what do we imagine he would expect
of us here and now? The question calls for a work of application,
interpretation, interpolation, imagination, and self-interrogation,
and all that is risky business. To interpret is always a high-wire
act, balancing oneself on a line stretched across an abyss and in
constant danger of constructing idols of its own imagining. The
name of "Jesus" is too often a mirror in which we behold our own
image, and it has always been easy to spot the sliver in the eye
of the other and miss the two-by-four in our own. The question
presupposes the inescapable reality of history and of historical
distance, and it asks how that distance can be crossed. Or better,
conceding that this distance cannot be crossed, the question resorts
to the subjunctive and asks how that irreducible distance could be
made creative. How does our distance from Jesus illuminate what
he said and did in a different time and place and under different
historical circumstances? And how does Jesus's distance from us
illuminate what we must say and do in the importantly different
situation in which we find ourselves today? The task of the church
is to submit *itself* to this question, rather than using it like a club
to punish others. The church, the archive of Jesus, in a very real
sense *is* this question. It has no other duty and no other privilege
than to bear this memory of Jesus and ask itself this question. The
church is not the answer. The church is the question, this question,
the gathering of people who are called together by the memory
of Jesus and who ask this question, who are called together and
are put into question by this question, who stand accused, under
the call, interrogated and unable to recuse themselves from this
question, and who come to understand that there are no easy,
ready-made, prepackaged answers.

The apostles "had hoped that the Kingdom of God would come,"
Alfred Loisy once famously remarked, but "what came was the
Church."[16] Let us call that statement Loisy's law. The arrival of the
church is a surprise—or what Derrida would call an event, meaning
something we do not see coming. The first followers of the Way
were expecting one event, an event to end all events, but they got
another, which really was a disappointment, a retrenchment, a
make do until the arrival of the kingdom, whose arrival has been
unexpectedly delayed. "Abbé" Loisy, who was an ex-priest, was

being cynical, but he makes a good point. The church is Plan B.[17] (In deconstruction, *everything* is Plan B.) The early church is a lot like the characters in the hit TV series *Lost*—the title is appropriate!—waiting to be "saved," which is the soteriological significance of that mysterious TV series where everyone is given a new being, a fresh start. At first, the survivors hang around on the beach waiting to get "picked up" (in a cloud, St. Paul said). After a while, they conclude that the rescue is not going to happen anytime soon and so they reluctantly decide to dig in and prepare for the long haul. Hence the existence of the church is provisional—like a long-term substitute teacher—praying for the kingdom, whose coming Jesus announced and which everyone was expecting would come some-time soon. But this coming was deferred, and the church occupies the space of the "deferral," of the distance or "difference," between two comings. (I just said, in case you missed it, the church is a function of *différance*!) In the meantime, and it is always the mean-time for the church, the church is supposed to do the best it can to bring that kingdom about in itself, here on earth, in a process of incessant self-renewal or auto-deconstruction, while not setting itself up as a bunch of kings or princes. The church is by definition a call (*kletos*) for renewal.

That is why the church is "deconstructible," but the kingdom of God, if there is such a thing, is not. The church is a provisional construction, and whatever is constructed is deconstructible, while the kingdom of God is that in virtue of which the church is de-constructible. So, if we ask, "What would Jesus deconstruct?" the answer is first and foremost the church! For the idea behind the church is to give way to the kingdom, to proclaim and enact and finally disappear into the kingdom that Jesus called for, all the while resisting the temptation of confusing itself with the kingdom. That requires us to clear away the rhetoric and get a clear picture of what "deconstruction" means, of just who "Jesus" is, and of the hermeneutic force of this "would," and to do so with this aim: to sketch a portrait of an alternative Christianity, one that is as ancient as it is new, one in which the "dangerous memory of Jesus" is still alive—deconstruction being, as I conceive it, a work of memory and imagination, of dangerous memories as well as daring ways to imagine the future, and as such good news for the church.

Spiritual Journeys, Postmodern Paths

> "I want to ask a question," said Rachel Winslow. . . . "Who is to decide for me just what He would do in my case? It is a different age. There are many perplexing questions in our civilization that are not mentioned in the teachings of Jesus. How am I going to tell what He would do?"
>
> "There is no way that I know of," replied the pastor, "except as we study Jesus through the medium of the Holy Spirit." . . .
>
> "Will it be possible to reach the same conclusions always in all cases?" asked President Marsh.
>
> Mr. Maxwell was silent some time. Then he answered, "No; I don't know that we can expect that."[1]
>
> —Sheldon, *In His Steps*
>
> "There is nothing outside the text."[2]
>
> —Jacques Derrida

In deconstruction, the figure of following "in his steps" is not repudiated but complicated; it is not jettisoned but given teeth.

Indeed, it is not too much to say that when Derrida penned the famous line "there is nothing outside the text" that sends the Right, religious and secular, into a deep swoon, he was saying that there is nothing outside the context of a text and therefore nothing that happens that does not follow in someone's steps, nothing that is not always and already inscribed within a network of tracks and traces of something or someone, known or unknown, avowed or unavowed, remembered or misremembered, for better or for worse. It is in recognition of this that Derrida usually formulates his own views not directly but by way of a commentary on a previous text, an old rabbinic practice, of course, but one that acknowledges we are always writing and thinking in the steps of a dense network of steps and texts, always following the "trace" of all that has preceded us. Far from denying the image of the steps, he would point out how many different footprints there are on this path and how difficult it is to make out just whose steps are whose.

Spiritual Journeys—Here and There

Over the ages the spiritual masters have described spiritual life as a journey. Indeed, we might even venture the thought that to be "religious" in its deepest sense is to be a searcher, living in search of something, as opposed to being satisfied with the reality that sits under our noses, content with the "present." When Bobby Kennedy used to say, "There are those who look at things the way they are, and ask why. . . . I dream of things that never were, and ask why not?" he was speaking with a religious heart.[3] Religious people are the people of the "why not?" the people of the promise, of the hope against hope. They restlessly search for something, for a certain sort of "transcendence," which means to be on the go, making a crossing, trying to get somewhere else. Saint Augustine might have been defining "religion" when he opened the *Confessions* with his famous reference to the *cor inquietum*, the "restless heart," which will not rest until it rests in "You," in what the great monotheistic religions call "God." Long before "Christians" knew what to call themselves, before the word "Christian" was coined, the earliest followers of Jesus were simply called followers of "the Way." To follow or be on the way may very well be what "religion" is—Lao Tzu spoke of the "Tao," meaning the "way"—the differences among religious traditions being worked out by their different visions of the way.[4] Seen thus, the way varies from the lowest, most self-aggrandizing, self-acquisitive, and heartless ways, where one makes a religion out of money or power, to the most sublime, inspiring, and heartfelt ways, which turn on love of the neighbor, compassion, hospitality, and forgiveness. In Christianity, Jesus is the way, and being a Christian cannot be more felicitously described than as following "in his steps." The religious heart or frame of mind is not "realist," because it is not satisfied with the reality that is all around it. Nor is it antirealist, because it is not trying to substitute fabrications for reality; rather, it is what I would call "hyper-realist," in search of the real beyond the real, the *hyper*, the *über* or *au-dèla*, the beyond, in search of the event that stirs within things that will exceed our present horizons. In this sense, religion is, in the very best and deepest sense, so much "hype."

We also are wont to think of life as an adventure. But a genuine adventure means venturing out into the unknown, where no one knows the way and we are not sure whose steps to follow. (Here comes the dose of postmodern truth, which will send my friends on the Right rushing for the doors.) Are we not all a little "lost," like the people who crash-landed on that island in *Lost*, looking for clues about where they are and frightened by the mysterious things going on around them? Is that not a figure of our lives? Are we not like people following an obscure clue, on the tracks, on the trail, in the trace of something-we-are-not-sure-what? Are not those who write about spiritual journeys sometimes a little too assured about where they are going and how to get there? There are, after all, two ways to be on the way: the first, in which one knows the way and the task is to get there (which certainly can be hard enough), and the second, in which one must, like an explorer, find the way. In the latter and, I am inclined to think, more postmodern situation, one is always a little lost, where being lost and being on the way, far from excluding each other, mutually imply each other. That is what I mean by giving the spiritual journey some postmodern teeth. I agree this is a little unnerving, but I do not agree that it is "relativism." Rather, it is what I just called "hyper-realism."

The sense of being "lost" I have in mind is confirmed by a simple test (which does not mean it is easy to pass), a little imaginative experiment devised by Edmund Husserl, the "father of phenomenology." The experience of the "other person," Husserl maintained, requires us to undertake what he called an "imaginative variation" to the effect that, *were I there*, "there" would become "here" for me and I would see things from that point of view.[5] Simply ask yourself what you would think and believe were you born "there," were "here" for you made of entirely different things, were you to wake up one fine day and find yourself in a very different time and place—the most extreme example of this is Gregor Samsa waking up as a cockroach in Kafka's *The Metamorphoses*—speaking a very different language, reading different books, having very different teachers, belonging to a very different culture. Would you still be you? How do you know who "you" are? Where do "you" begin and all the saturating influences of culture and education leave off? Is not the first step in self-knowledge to concede that we do not know who we are? When we go to church on Sunday morning and join hands and sing communal songs and recite the ancient prayers of the community, must we not ask ourselves what it would be like were we joining other hands in some other community, singing other songs, and saying other prayers at other times in other traditions where the way is different, where they (which has now become *we*) would follow different ways? Were you "there," and were everyone there agreed about following "in his steps," that would mean following someone different, following a very different way, but all with the same heartfelt conviction and deep faith of the "here." That is our common situation and the basis of a common understanding and compassion.

If truth be told, we should all be a little spooked by that thought, a little haunted that there are no hooks to lift us above that "situatedness" or "contextuality." Let us call this the "hauntological" principle, in virtue of which to be on a spiritual journey is to be a little spooked by the radical contingency of our situation, individual or communal. So what I mean by being "lost" is not wandering aimlessly but recognizing the contingency of the network of steps, tracks, and traces within which we find ourselves, conceding the contingency of what we call "here" and the multiplicity of other "heres" that are over "there." That requires the ability to imagine ourselves otherwise and hence to concede that while we firmly embrace the idea of the rock of ages, different ages rest on different rocks.

Given the firmly entrenched view among many evangelical Christians that postmodernists are people with visions of nihilism dancing in their heads, I am sure this all sounds bad to my friends (s'il y en a) on the Christian Right. But I am simply trying to give the idea of a spiritual journey some bite, some postmodern wisdom teeth, if you will. I am not recommending nihilism. I am simply pointing out the plain sense of the plurality of things, the plain sense of the geographical and historical contingency of our lives. I know about treating contingency as grace, and I am getting to that. But first, if truth be told, and let us assume we are all trying to tell the truth, I maintain that no one really *knows* the way, not in any deep-down epistemologically unshakeable way, although we all have, and must have, our several faiths—multiple communities of faiths shaped by centuries of experience—each with great theological, liturgical, and ethical practices and traditions. On my accounting we are not preprogrammed or hardwired to the Truth (otherwise we would not be free) but proceed perforce by one form of faith or another, more often than not the one in which we find ourselves. The reason we are on a journey, the reason we have our several faiths, the reason the early Christians and Lao Tzu speak of following a "way," is precisely the contingency and givenness of the world in which we find ourselves and the desire we have for a guide. If we were not lost, if we were just hardwired to a spiritual global positioning system, we would not need to be saved. We must appreciate that we are lost before being "found" or being "saved" makes any sense.

The spiritual journey on which we are embarked is, we say, a journey of *faith*. That means that those who insist they *know* the way have programmed their lives, have put their lives on automatic pilot. They are knowers (gnostics) who have taken themselves out of the game. They are like vacationers eager for an adventure, to set forth into the unknown—but not without an air-conditioned Hummer with four-wheel drive, an experienced guide, and reservations at a five-star hotel. Indeed, even were we able to hook up to a satellite system that would guide our travels around the physical globe, still, for radical spiritual sojourners like us, this earthly globe is but a speck of dust in an infinite universe, and we keep asking where it is all going.

So we ought not to undertake the project posed by Sheldon's book, indeed by 1 Peter 2:21—the task of following "in his steps"—too lightly or in such a way as to think that we have thereby been insulated from the wider human adventure, from the human condition. Jesus is not the way unless you are lost, even as Jesus is not the answer unless you have a question. I am happy enough to call this the "postmodern condition," to use Lyotard's phrase. If that much-abused phrase still means anything at all—I myself use it mainly to draw a crowd—I take it to mean the condition of irreducible pluralism. We live in a world of instant global communication, linked by satellite communication systems to the most remote corners of the world, which exposes us at every turn to a plurality of voices and choices, races and places, cultures and religions, to the multiplicity of lifestyles and ways to be. The very phrase "lifestyles" says it all. Where once we might have spoken of "wisdom" or "the good life," today we leave as much space as possible for multiple wisdoms and goods, all in the plural. So, in the postmodern world, the first question anybody would ask on being presented with a book titled *In His Steps* is, "In *whose* steps?" And what about *in her steps*? Or suppose, like Frank Sinatra, I want to do it "my way"? In the postmodern situation, the very idea of a "spiritual journey" seems to suggest that there is more than one, that each of us must find a way, which itself presumes that we are all a bit lost.

The Step/Not Beyond

It is thus not surprising that the dominant figure of Sheldon's classic, and the one that frames the question "What would Jesus do?"—the figure of the "step"—is an important topic among postmodern writers. It is especially important in deconstruction where this figure functions quite radically, so much so that it seems at first blush to flatly contradict Sheldon's use of it. Instead of the trope of leading and following in the steps of a sure guide, the "step" in deconstruction has to do with interrupted passages and missteps. It is a peculiarity of French—and the French theorists take advantage of this—that the word for step, *pas*, means both "step," as in *faux pas*, when we make a false step, and "not," as in *je ne sais pas*, "I don't know." At first this appears to be just an oddity of the French language, an idiom, a completely untranslatable play on words, of no consequence outside of French, and more evidence in favor of the Righteous Denunciators of Deconstruction Inc., which has often accused Derrida of playing with words instead of thinking clearly. Apart from replying that "thou art Peter and on this Rock I will build my church" is also a play on words and that Jesus himself seems to be no small verbal master, allow me to insist that there is more to it than that.[6] *Pas* is the kind of word Derrida likes, what he calls an "undecidable," which means that it fluctuates but *in an instructive way* (not arbitrarily) between two different and sometimes even opposed meanings.[7] Thus *pas* means "step/not"; it means to take a step but then again not to, to be following in someone's steps but then again not to. Steps cannot be insulated in an absolute way from missteps and sidesteps, and paths cannot be protected from dead ends. To take steps in a certain direction, to be en route, to follow in someone's steps, cannot be protected absolutely from detours, road blocks, misleading road signs, false steps, and impasses, just the sorts of things that Sheldon's characters were worried about. So if we let ourselves be put in question by this question, we will ask ourselves if we are indeed following in his steps or just going where we want to go on our own.

But if Sheldon's book could play well in Kansas with a title like *In His Steps*, the great twentieth-century German philosopher Martin Heidegger could write a famous book called *Holzwege*, which means making one's way along barely discernible "forest paths" and which has recently been translated as *Off the Beaten Track*, while Maurice Blanchot, a formidably difficult French writer and theorist, could write a book called *Le Pas au-delà*, which, as you can see, is a bit of a challenge to translate.[8] On the one hand, that title means "the step beyond," and hence signifies "transcendence," entering another sphere, which as we have seen goes to the very heart of a spiritual journey that itself is nothing if it is not a search for transcendence, for the "beyond." That's the part that makes religious hearts glow and has led Christian painters to portray the saints with those unctuous looks directed heavenward. It is also an ancient philosophical trope, going back to climbing the steep ascent out of Plato's famous cave to the upper sun-lit world, taking the "step beyond" the sensible world of appearances to the real world of the unchanging forms, which Plato described as going "beyond being."[9] But on the other hand, this title means "the 'no beyond,'" "no transcendence," "no trespassing," or even "no religion!"—as in "no smoking" (*pas de fumer*). So the English translator just gave in and translated it *The Step Not Beyond*. In colloquial English today we might translate it, with a bit of a smirk, *Transcendence—Not*!

I will not swear that Blanchot was not trying to torment us half to death, but I will say that even if he was he was making an important point. Take, for example, the ethical respect we owe the "other person," which on Blanchot's terms is a paradigm of the step/not beyond. As Emmanuel Levinas (an equally formidable French writer) said, the other person is a shore we will never reach, another side for which we set sail in our little crafts but one on which we never actually arrive, a point that also goes back to Husserl. (Blanchot and Levinas were lifelong friends, perhaps because they were among the few who understood what the other was talking about.) Our relationship with the other person is a real relation—we encounter the other "in person," "in the flesh." That is the "proximity" of two persons, which goes to the heart of ethics and has preoccupied French philosophy for the last three decades. But this proximity is infiltrated with "distance" so that this very real relation is also really a relation "without relation" in the sense that the other person is constituted by an interiority or an interior secret that we can never access, a secret inner self that we can never really reach or know. (Only God knows what is in the heart of each of us.) Hence the "distance-in-proximity" (the step/not beyond) is constitutive of the experience of another person. The other person is really encountered but the true reality of the other is a hyper-reality to which we never gain access. We can lift the lid of a music box and look inside to see what was hidden from our view, or look inside a clock to see what makes it tick, but we can never really look inside the mind and heart of another person. We just can never get there. The other person is not one of our possibilities but one of our impossibilities. Below I will also point out what you might have already begun to suspect: the step/not beyond is also a splendid image of what theology calls the *via negativa*, in which the "way" (*via*) to God is marked by the "not" that draws a zone of absolute respect around the transcendence of God. If you comprehend it, Augustine said, it is not God.

The relation with the other person is therefore a journey we never complete, where that incompleteness is not an imperfection but testimony to the perfect excess of the other; it is not a loss but a source of endless novelty and discovery. Were the opposite true, our relation to the other would be ruined (an important philosophical point that is spoofed in the Mel Gibson film *What Women Want*). We can never be sure of what is going on in the heart of the other but we affirm that distance rather than being demoralized or defeated by it. The relation to the other is bracing but risky business. To give a very concrete example of what I mean, when you get married, you are saying "I do" not only to who this person *is*, or who you think this person is, but to whomever or whatever this person is going to *become*, which is unknown and unforeseen to the both of you. That is a risk, what Levinas called a "beautiful risk," but it is a risk all the same, at best a fifty-fifty chance if we can go by the divorce rates. But the risk is *constitutive* of the vow or the commitment. It is the faith these two people have in each other that we admire, the willingness to go forward, even though the way is not certain, that leads us to describe it as beautiful. If it were a sure thing, it would be about as beautiful as a conversation with your stockbroker. (You can also see—and here the faces of the Right will redden—that we have gone a long way toward defining the essence of a personal vow without ever having said a thing about opposing genders!)

So we start to see how deeply the *not* is embedded in the *path*, how deeply the impasse is embedded in the pass, and more generally how deeply the impossible is embedded in the possible—almost to the point that, far from being a simple play on words among wild-eyed French theorists, it is beginning to look like a *law*, and indeed one very close to the religious heart. Think about faith, hope, and charity singled out by St. Paul. When is faith really faith? Not when it is looking more and more like we are right, but when the situation is beginning to look impossible, in the darkest night of the soul. The more credible things are, the less faith is needed, but the more incredible things seem, the more faith is required, the faith that is said to move mountains. So, too, hope is hope not when we have every reason to expect a favorable outcome, which is nothing more than a reasonable expectation (the virtue of a stockbroker), but when it is beginning to look hopeless, when we are called on to "hope against hope," as St. Paul says (Rom.

4:18), which is a magnificently deconstructive turn of phrase. This is above all true of love, where loving those who are lovable or those who love you makes perfect sense. But when is love really love? When does love burn white hot? When we love those who are *not* lovable or who do *not* love us—in short, when we love our enemies. In other words, we are really on the way of faith and hope and love when the way is blocked; we are really under way when the way seems impossible, where this "impossible" makes the way possible.[10] It is precisely the "not" that makes the "path" kick into high gear.

Part of my hypothesis in this little book is that deconstruction and the kingdom of God—I have invested a lot of my time as a professional philosopher trying to set up a shuttle system between these two—are marked by a common love of paradox and aporia and by a common appreciation of the path, not as a well-paved, well-marked superhighway but as an obstructed path, a step/not, a movement of the beyond, of excess, and ultimately of the madness of love.

Lost Mail, Dead Ends, Impasses—and Affirmation

Thus while his conservative critics charge that Derrida is trying to lead us into temptation, we should be able to see that all this emphasis on the "not" does not mean that Derrida is being negative. Derrida is not an obstructionist but a deconstructionist, and deconstruction is affirmation—affirmation of memory and the future, of the past and of what is coming, and of how to be on the move. Derrida is pointing out that the possibility of the misstep or the false step is constitutive of the step, that it is built right into it. The misstep is a condition of the possibility of the step, part of its risk and part of its creativity, something like a creative misunderstanding. The possibility of going astray is, as he would say, a "structural" matter, in just the same way that it is always possible for a word to be misunderstood. It was with this in mind that Derrida wrote a book early on called *The Post Card*, which was organized around the figure of the possibility of lost mail, the structural possibility that a letter *may not arrive at its destination*.[11] On the cover of this important book was a reproduction of a medieval painting on a "postcard" found in the book shop of the Bodleian Library in Oxford, which appeared to be a representation of Socrates seated at a writing desk while Plato whispered like a little bird in his ear. That reverses the line of influence between teacher and disciple, but it also reflects the fact that Plato, who was a writer of magisterial proportions, fed Socrates, who never wrote a thing, some of his best lines in his "Dialogues." Of course, that is exactly what any historical-critical scholar of the New Testament will tell you about the relationship between the authors of the New Testament and some of the best lines of Jesus, who also never wrote a thing.

Derrida "literally" meant a "letter" in the post, but more figuratively or generally he meant a text, a work of "literature," and the very structure of writing, *écriture* or *scriptura* (sacred or not so sacred), and in the widest sense of the whole "web" of institutions and practices, the whole network of steps, tracks, and traces. *The Post Card* was an economic figure for saying several different things. On one level, Derrida meant that a text—say, one of the letters written by St. Paul—is a physical object and it may get lost (as were most of the letters of Paul and all of the first manuscripts of the Gospels) or misquoted or altered over several centuries of editing (which has also happened to the Scriptures).[12] He also meant that a text simply may not be understood by its recipients, who never "get" what is "sent." Finally, he meant that even when it is not lost and even when it is understood, a text remains structurally and in principle capable of being understood *differently*—by different communities of readers at different times, in other times and other places—so that it is always happening (*arriver*) but never arrives (*arriver*) decisively at just one final destination (I will come back to this point below) that would be authorized to pronounce its meaning once and for all.[13]

Christianity is a good example of the postal principle in several ways, for in Christianity the Hebrew Scriptures arrived in a place they did not see coming and were made to say things by the authors of the New Testament that favored a Christian outcome. The authors of the New Testament were not "fundamentalists" about reading the Hebrew Scriptures but were very creative readers and misreaders of those ancient texts. They had their own agenda. Furthermore, the postal system very much governs the subsequent Christian tradition and the fate of a question like "What would Jesus do?" which is a question that each Christian individually and the church collectively keeps posing and re-posing to itself. The Christian tradition *itself*—the postal principle is the principle of any tradition—is the history of taking the story of Jesus differently, again and again, over the course of the ages, in changing times and circumstances. It is everywhere itself and everywhere different. It keeps saying new things.

This is a point of which Sheldon himself was not innocent. "How are we supposed to know what Jesus would do?" Rachel Winslow asks. What are we to do about the fact that there are different interpretations of what he would do? Is this not a very different time? How can we be sure the "good news" is delivered to or arrives at its destination? Nothing is guaranteed by a literal reproduction of what Jesus did, which would make no sense; we need instead a creative reproduction, a creative repetition, a repetition with a difference. So the upshot of deconstruction is not to shoot down Sheldon's question but to unfold its depths and complexity, to supply its hermeneutics.

While Sheldon was not unaware of the complications, his emphasis falls more on whether we have the courage to follow the plain and obvious model that Jesus provides—to love our enemies, to sell what we have and give it to the poor—rather than on having the wisdom or insight to sort out just how this model can be realized in the complexity of our present situation. To be sure, would that we could ever get as far as Sheldon asked! We have a map, someone to lead the way, but the real challenge is to follow it, to summon up the courage to walk "in his steps." But suppose the original map is old and there has been a lot of construction and development since then and shifting tides have redrawn the coast so that all the markers on the map have been obscured. So in deconstruction, the "step" is a more unsettled and confusing business, and we are always a little more lost, more adrift, or as Derrida says, *destinerrant*. This is a neologism—Derrida is an avant-garde writer and so he uses a lot of neologisms—meaning to be of erring or straying destiny, or perhaps to be destined to stray or wander off course. However, "errancy" does not mean utterly aimless, hopeless wandering. Rather, human life is to be compared to the "knights errant," not only knights who are on an "errand" in quest of something, but also knights who get lost, who lose a lot of time riding around in circles and occasionally falling off their horses, which in the case of St. Paul represented decisive progress. In deconstruction, to be under way is neither a matter of following a well-marked way, as it often is for Sheldon, nor a matter of setting out on more uncharted forest paths, as it is for Heidegger. Rather, it is a matter of following paths that have been so heavily traveled that there is a confusing plethora of tracks and we are not sure whose steps are whose.

You can get a sense of the sort of path that postmodernists have in mind by giving a deconstructive analysis of the religious idea of having a "vocation," which means to follow the call that directs our spiritual journey. It should be clear that by a deconstruction I mean an analysis that shows something is possible—here a "vocation"—only under conditions that also block it or make it impossible (like hoping against hope or loving the unlovable).[14] A vocation means to be "called," to live "under" a call—but suppose we are not sure who the caller of the call is? Is the voice that calls to us in conscience the call of God? Or is it perhaps a kind of evolutionary device implanted by the process of natural selection? You can see how much being called, living *under* a call, or being called or summoned to follow a call is affected by "identifying" who the caller is. That is exactly what Kant, who wanted a religion of pure reason and pure autonomy, objected to in the story of the binding of Isaac—before obeying this call Abraham should have asked more questions about the identity of this voice that commanded such a horrific thing. But to the extent that one actually knows or can identify the caller, the sender of this mail, one gets *on top of* the call and can judge *for oneself* about the validity of what is called for. And to that extent one is less under the call and more in possession of one's own faculties, more autonomous. One is acting on one's own—not under the call. (Much like the way "caller ID" restores our autonomy by getting us out from under the disruption telephone calls cause us by allowing us to decide for ourselves if and when to respond to a "call.") So you see that the spiritual journey we launch under the impetus of a calling or vocation (the path) actually depends on *not* knowing whence this call arises, on not knowing who has sent this mail, and thus on not entirely understanding what is being called for. That is also why it is important to stay under the call of the question of what Jesus would do—put in the accusative, called into question by the question—and not try to get on top of it and wield it like a stick. We have a sense, a faith, a hope in something, a love of

something we know not what, something that calls on us. The
great dignity of being human lies in pursuing goals for which
there is no guarantee of success and even, at a certain point, no
hope of success. But being "religious people," by which I mean
people who dream of things that have never been and ask "why
not?" we still pursue them.[15]

Counterpaths

I like to think of Derrida as the author of a complicated version
of a certain Augustine, not the orthodox bishop, of course, but a
kind of Jewish and, well, postmodern Augustine—not so much
Augustine the bishop but the Augustine of the *cor inquietum* in the
Confessions.[16] Like Augustine, Derrida was born in North Africa
and was resolved to make it in the Big Apple (Paris, not Rome).
He was a constant traveler, though he professed hating it, flying
all over the world to teach and lecture about deconstruction and
doing a lot of his writing on airplanes and in hotel rooms. This is a
function of being a philosopher in the jet age, a thing not possible
for Augustine or Kant. But it is more than that. He was a *homo
viator* in a deeper sense, a man ever under way, a "restless heart,"
almost as if he did not have a home, or only one home, which is
nearly the same thing. Catherine Malabou recently collaborated
with Derrida on a book titled *Counterpath: Traveling with Jacques
Derrida*.[17] The book tells us a lot about Derrida's childhood in Alge-
ria and life on the *rue Saint Augustin*, and it is a good example of
Derrida's love of experimental writing, of writing in such a way as
to "produce an event." It consists, on the one hand, of a "running"
commentary written by Malabou on Derrida and, on the other
hand, of "postcards" written "on the run," from various points of
travel, by Derrida, who did not know what Malabou, back home
in Paris, was writing about him. Then the two authors put their
texts together to see what sort of convergences, divergences, and
questions arose, to see what sort of sparks they set off, to see if
they set off an event.[18] Malabou expounds Derrida's thought by
settling into the undecidability of the French words *dériver* and
arriver. *Dériver* signifies at one and the same time "to derive" but
also "to drift" or "to deviate," while *arriver* means not only to arrive
at or reach the destination one has consciously set out to reach

but also to come about by chance, to happen, like a surprise (as in the surprise ending given to a lot of Hebrew Scriptures in the New Testament). Since in deconstruction everything turns on "the coming of the event," or the "advent of the other," the emphasis falls on drift and surprise, the incalculability, the errancy, which turns garden-variety voyages into radical ventures into the unknown—into real trips!

We have already seen an example of this when we considered the felicitous ambiguity of *pas*, which is a happy chance, a piece of luck (but it has a historical basis). Derrida likes to settle into these pieces of luck and explore their richness. Just in case this is making you nervous, remember that in theology we call such felicity a "grace" and that deconstruction is very interested in the gift of a grace or the grace of a gift. One of the most momentous events in the history of Christianity turns on exactly such a piece of luck, chance, felicity, or grace: the conversion of St. Augustine. Augustine tells us that one day, by chance, he heard children playing a game, *"tolle, lege,"* which he took as a sign from God to take and read the book of Scripture that happened to be in Latin and an arm's length away from him at the time and to take to heart whatever passage his eye fell on, on whatever page he happened to open. When he did that, his eye fell on the words of St. Paul in Romans 13:13—and the rest is history, namely the history of Christian theology in the Western church.[19] Derrida would only add to this the suggestion that you have to watch out for gifts, because gifts can poison. That is a bilingual pun (whence his interest in James Joyce), which does not mean it is not important; *die Gift*, in German, means poison, so *die Gift vergiftet* could mean "the gift poisons." Once again, there is a parallel in theology, which says the same thing about gifts when it warns us to be careful what you pray for—you may get it.

So it is not a pure accident that a lot of Derrida's books reflect his travels and the motif of travel, not the travels of the *Odyssey*, where the hero eventually makes a circle and comes home, but more Jewish and uprooted travels, like Abraham's, where the hero answers a call that uproots him from his home, never to come back again. In deconstruction, you hear a lot of Jewish things along with Greek and philosophical things, a lot about exile, diaspora, dissemination, difference, and what Derrida, after Levinas, called the "wholly other" (*tout autre*), with which he also has a link to

Husserl.[20] As we have been thinking of deconstruction as a philosophy of the voyage, which in religious literature is called a spiritual journey, think of Derrida as also a kind of deconstructive St. Paul, traveling all over the known world, sending back letters to the churches, and like Paul getting shipwrecked, jailed, bitten by a snake, and run out of a lot of towns as a heretic. The idea is to deconstruct the garden-variety idea of travel or voyaging, of being under way, which involves the passage from a clear starting point to a goal or end known clearly in advance, along with the sure means of getting from one place to the other. In the deconstruction of the voyage, or the voyage taken deconstructively, one is more *creatively adrift*, which is the condition of an "invention," in the literal sense of the breaking in (*in-venire*), the "incoming" (in the military sense!) of something unforeseeable, which defines life's "adventure" (*ad-venire*). We start out in a situation of indecipherable complexity and we are not so sure where we are heading, much less how to get there. Catherine Keller, one of the leading American theologians of the day, helpfully compares deconstruction on this point to chaos theory, which describes how a certain optimal state of chaos must be an ingredient in a system if the system is to be productive.[21] Not simple chaos, not flat out anarchy, which produces nothing, but what James Joyce (again!) called a "chaosmos," a chaos-in-cosmos, an ordered disorder, where the tension between the two is set in a delicate balance that allows the system to generate new and unforeseen effects. I think Jesus caused disturbances like that, shaking up the system, opening up new and dangerous possibilities.

If you knew very well where you were going from the start and had the means to get there, it would almost be like getting there before you even set out or like ending up where you were all along, which is what postmodernists call the "future present." The result would be nothing new—no surprise, no discovery, no "event," and no advent of the other, or not much of one. Real journeys are full of unexpected turns and twists, requiring a faith that can move mountains and a hope against hope, where one does not see what one was trying to do until the journey is completed, which postmodernists call the "absolute future." Deconstruction, like the Christianity of Kierkegaard's Johannes Climacus, is not a Platonic "recollection," a getting back to where you already were or a recovering of a possession that you did not realize you possessed all along. It is not a matter of becoming who you already are but of becoming something new, a *metanoia*, a new creation, which eye has not seen nor ear heard nor the heart imagined, an openness to the coming of the other, which we don't already possess. Thus, in a deconstructive analysis, you could never simply "derive" an idea or a practice from its "sources," as if it were already implicitly there. It does not flow from its "origin" as a more or less inevitable conclusion. It comes by way of an unexpected turn of events, by shattering our horizon of expectation. So when we go back to the New Testament, to any classic text or constitution, we cannot hope to simply and straightforwardly "derive" instruction from it, as if we could simply run a computer program on it. We must instead allow it to happen (*arriver*) to us, which in theology has to do with what the Rev. Maxwell called "the medium of the Holy Spirit" (*In His Steps*, 18).

Derrida's *cor inquietum*, his own path of thought or "journey"— his whole life was a journey—proceeds without him ever seeing clearly where he was going. If he could see in advance (fore-see, *pro-videre*) where he was headed, that would in an important sense vitiate the journey, rob it of its eventiveness, rob the e-vent of its ad-venture. Deconstruction is adventure, is risky business, as is life. So life and deconstruction go hand in hand (wherever they are going). Going to a place we already know how to reach, or going with a tour guide who has mapped out every stop along the way, or along a paved road with guard rails, rest stops, and food stands where everyone speaks English, is hardly a journey at all. When Derrida visited a city, he did not like to be "shown around"; he liked to go off on his own and get "lost" in the city. The most authentic journeys are explorations in which I really do not know what I am going to find—once again like the characters in *Lost*, who set out on an exploration of their island with a great deal of trepidation because *with each step* they do not know what to expect. The jungle in *Lost* is very spooky. It is being lost that gives the survivors' journeys around that jungle its teeth. Each step they take on that island is full of apprehension, excitement, discovery, and suspense, which is, of course, a clever premise for a TV series that wants to be sure its viewers tune in next week. (I read once that the script writers of *Casablanca* kept just a few days ahead of the production schedule, and the result was unforgettable.) One can admire the good and faithful servant who sticks to the well-trod path, but it is quite another thing to know that with each step I might step into a trap, be attacked by a monster—or have my whole life transformed.

Indeed, is it not a heresy in Christianity to assert that we *know* what we are doing and can do so very well by ourselves, thank you very much? The *pas au-delà* is in fact a venerable figure in theology. To set out for a shore that we can never reach, to be exposed to a secret we can never plumb—what is that if not a description of a proper path to God? (Remember, Derrida and Levinas are Jewish writers and the transcendence of God and the critique of idols are in their bones.) The logic of the *pas* is played out in an exemplary way in mystical or negative theology, which very straight-laced theologians with no taste for puns (as well as mystical poets who delight in puns) call the *via negativa*. And what is the *via negativa* if not the way or path marked by the not, the passage to a shore we will never reach, a step/not beyond? Why can I not stop speaking of God, of whom I cannot say a thing? The path to God is also a counterpath, where a great "not" inscribes a zone of absolute respect around "God," meaning, among other things, that we should be very cautious about pronouncing what "God" is or means lest we find ourselves falling down before an idol. The same caution is required of pronouncing what Jesus would do, which is beset by the same confusion.

Life is a journey, a "spiritual journey," a "forest path" (Heidegger's *Holzweg*), a "counterpath" (Derrida's *contre-allée*), a *via negativa* (mystical theology). A genuine journey is open ended, and it makes itself open to the gift of chance (Derrida), to the grace of the moment, or to the prompting of the Spirit (theology), as Saints Paul and Augustine believed. Resolution is not the same as rigidity.[22] We proceed with no preconceived conclusions and we are prepared to surrender to the Spirit, to be guided whither it will lead, including places we do not want to go (*especially* to places we do not want to go). That is one way to define prayer. You might even say, with a perfectly straight face, that Derrida's "hauntology," which is a philosophy of the spirit, of a very deconstructive s(S)pirit, is written in a s(S)pirit of prayer, in the same way the *Confessions* of Augustine are a great prayer. From time to time Derrida himself has signaled that when deconstruction is understood in the most searching manner possible it finds itself indistinguishably close to a state that in religion is called prayer, which is his deeply Augustinian streak, his version of *coram deo*. To pray is to adopt a certain posture, a way to stand before God, exposed *to* God *by* God, *à dieu*, in which God is the possibility of the impossible, the "wholly other," the unforeseeable, the one who breaks down our egological and monological preoccupations and exposes us to the coming of the other, the incoming of what we did not see coming. The true journey means that there is something unknown and unknowable, unforeseeable and impossible, and hence a little frightening about following the Spirit. If that is so, as I believe it is, then even the religious path we follow if we dare ask ourselves what Jesus would do, the *imitatio Christi*, is every bit as much a counterpath. The characters in *In His Steps* do not make their pledge lightly, and they are more than a little anxious about where their pledge is going to lead them and about the profound and unforeseeable transformations that lay in store for them:

> No man can tell until he is moved by the Divine Spirit what he may do, or how he may change the current of a lifetime of fixed habits of thought and speech and action. Henry Maxwell did not, as we have said, yet know himself all that he was passing through, but he was conscious of a great upheaval in his definition of Christian discipleship, and he was moved with a depth of feeling he could not measure as he looked into the faces of those men and women on this occasion. (*In His Steps*, 17)

The essential path is beset by the counterpath, which does not undo the path but makes it possible. The counterpath haunts the path; deconstruction describes the ghosts that haunt us, the spirits that inspire us, and the difficulty of discerning among these several spirits. Deconstruction "itself"—I do not actually think there is any such thing—is not a determinate position, a definite "what" or worldview with a manifesto, or a platform or a set of positions, theistic or atheistic, but a "how," a *way* of holding a position, of being under way or being on a path. It is an affirmation without being a self-certain and positive position. It does not occupy a position of opposition to Christianity or to any other concrete or determinate belief or practice. Deconstruction is rather more of a ghost, adding a specter to the Spirit whose lead we are trying to follow. It provides an unsettling reminder about how to hold any given position, about how not (*pas*) to hold any given position, about not holding it in too settled a way with too much complacency and self-assurance, and about allowing ourselves to be held.

Deconstruction describes the common human condition that besets us all, and if we want to call that our postmodern condition, we should remember that it is also very ancient. We human beings, *homo viator*, are travelers all, journeying along an obscure route, and so depending for all our lives on receiving hospitality along the way and compassion for our common lot. That is exactly the situation of that wayfaring fellow who showed up that Sunday morning at the doors of the First Church of Raymond, Kansas, and who died from neglect a few days later in Rev. Henry Maxwell's home, whose Christian hospitality proved too little too late. ("Lord, when did we see you hungry and give you something to eat?")

Now my point in all this is not to make trouble for the sake of making trouble but to tell the truth, the postmodern truth, to put some teeth into the idea of a spiritual journey, and to get a realistic, nay a more hyper-realistic, portrait of our common condition. If truth be told, is this not a fairer figure of our lives? Is this not a more compassionate and merciful account of who we are, of everyone, "here" and "there"?

3

A Prayer for the Impossible

A Catechumen's Guide to Deconstruction

As we have just seen, one of the things Derrida means by a text or a tradition is that it keeps "happening" (*arriver*) without ever quite "arriving" at a final, fixed, and finished destination. We cannot simply "derive" (*dériver*) direct instruction from it, but we must instead allow it a certain drift or free play (*dérive*), which allows that tradition to be creative and reinvent itself so that it can be, as Augustine said of God, ever ancient yet ever new. That, as I pointed out, does not scuttle the figure of walking "in the steps" of someone, but it does give it some teeth. I said in the first chapter that I am presenting the New Testament as a "poetics" of the kingdom of God, a theo-poetics—as opposed to a "theo-logic," an ethics, or a church dogmatics—as a complex of narratives, parables, and paradoxes of which Jesus is the centerpiece. From a work such as that we cannot simply and straightforwardly "derive" a course of action. We need instead to "arrive" at an instantiation, a concretization, a way to translate it into existence, all the while letting it happen (*arriver*) to us, allowing ourselves to come under its spell and be transformed by the event it harbors. For that we require a delicate style of interpretation, a "hermeneutics," which is the role played here by deconstruction, which I am presenting as the hermeneutics of the kingdom of God.

To that end I want to sketch out in this chapter some features of the slightly Jewish-Augustinian reading I am giving of Derrida, according to which deconstruction can be seen—not without controversy—as a form of prayer. In the view I take of deconstruction, we are constantly praying for something that has already happened but is always arriving, for something remembered but also promised, for something nameless that goes under many names, something that overtakes us and draws us out of ourselves. Among the many names under which deconstruction travels, I number "justice," the "gift," "forgiveness," and "hospitality" as the most important to our present purposes. These I will treat below as incognitos of "*the* impossible."

The Vocativeness of Events

I begin with a distinction between events—something that has already happened but is still arriving—and the names or things in which events are expressed. Allow me to illustrate this distinction with an anecdote. I once attended a conference in which a theologian who (like God, he will be nameless), not liking Jacques Derrida very much (I could tell), asked the audience, or rather, quite indignantly intoned as from on high, "Can God be deconstructed?" I ventured a reply—to his surprise, I think, because he did not really expect anyone to answer, he being of the opinion that he had with this question thereby deconstructed deconstruction (by which he meant reduced it to rubble). I allowed that while I hesitated to speak for God, it was certainly true that the *name* of God can and should be deconstructed. Indeed, I would go so far as to say that the long history of "theology" (which, however venerable a name, has like the rest of us to stay on guard against *hybris*) has been an ongoing work of deconstructing the name of God in order to release the *event* that stirs within that name. On that point we may all be well instructed by the respect shown for this name in the Jewish tradition. Furthermore, although this is another point, one of the difficulties that theologies of any stripe must face is that the event that stirs within the name of God can take place under other names, which complicates the distinction between theism and atheism.

So, then, what is an event? Let us start by saying that events are not names or things but something going on *in* names or things, and it is that special something that commands the particular attention of deconstruction.[1] Think of the event as first of all a simmering potency in a name, a possibility that inhabits the name, what that name is trying to express while never quite succeeding, something that the name recalls but never quite remembers, promises but never quite delivers. When we respond to the event in a name we not only respond to what it "actually" refers to, but we are also being provoked by what it promises or recalls. One of Derrida's favorite examples in this regard is the name "democracy." He once wrote an essay that cited Montaigne: "Oh my fellow democrats, there are no democrats."[2] The ever-righteous Right, which has a tin ear for Derrida, gets up in arms when Derrida says things like that, and it self-righteously proclaims, again from on high (I think they must carry portable folding pulpits with them), the difference between the Western democracies and, say, the Nazis or the old Soviet Union. But that is rather a flatfooted and unpoetic way to take what Derrida meant. Kierkegaard could very well have stood up in church some Sunday morning and said to his fellow Danes, "Oh my fellow Christians, there are no Christians," by which he was not remarking that the Danes had all recently become Hindus. Anyone who hears what is resonating in the word "democracy" (or "Christianity"), anyone with an ear for its poetics, for what it promises and recalls, knows that no existing democracy, nothing that dares call itself a democracy today, is up to what is called for in that name. When we call something by a name like "democracy," something is being called for, something is being recalled and promised, an event of democracy, that, as the Scriptures might put it, eye has not seen nor ear heard. When we speak of something (say the United States) being "worthy of the name" (say, democracy), we are speaking of the event that name contains. The event that is going on *in* the name is the event of a *call*, of something calling and of something being called for *by* the name. The event has the structure of a call (and a re-call) while the name is a kind of shelter or temporary housing for the event. Let us say that the event belongs to the "vocative" order—the order of what is calling, what is called for, what is recalled, and who is called on—while names and things belong to the "existential" order, the order of what actually exists, of natural languages and real things.

Democracy, or rather the event that is "harbored" (which means both protected and hidden) in the name "democracy," is what is coming, as the "democracy to come." The event is unconditional because it is the promise of something that is never realized under the existing conditions in which things are actually found. This is an idea that Derrida has borrowed not from Plato but from Judaism, which is why he calls it the "pure messianic" form, not an "ideal" form. But be aware that he has in mind a slightly peculiar idea of the "Messiah," found in some rabbinic traditions, where the Messiah never actually shows up, where the Messiah is the name of the pure structure of hope and expectation. In that understanding, if the Messiah did show up he would ruin everything, for then there would be no future, which is a way of saying that history would be over. That point is well illustrated by the history of Christianity, in which, since it is believed that the Messiah has already come, its history consists in waiting for him to come *again*. Originally, Christianity was not supposed to have a history because the Messiah had come. There wasn't even supposed to be such a thing as Christianity. The "history of Christianity" opens only with the delay that came about when Jesus failed to come (again)—the church being the temporary shelter that has been built in the meantime (Plan B). So even if the Messiah has already come, that would not satisfy us, for as long as we live in time and history, among the deconstructibles, we will want him to come *again*! The structure of the "to come," symbolized by the empty chair that is set for Elijah, is a structure of openness to the future, to what may come knocking at our door. On this Jewish analogy, it would be "idolatrous" to identify the event of something like democracy with its present state of affairs—the current conditions under which it is found being like the golden calf—instead of being drawn by the call of that event toward an open-ended future.

But we should not be misled by this stress on the "to come" into thinking that the temporality of the call, or the historicity of the event, is one-sidedly futural, as if we were just dreaming about something that will never be. Remember what we said above about the dangerous memories of the suffering of the dead. Deconstruction is a way to dream, and dreaming is important, as Martin Luther King Jr. made perfectly plain. But deconstruction is not only a dream, and it is not only about the future. As a "call" or solicitation, the event is no less a memory, a call back, a re-call to the past that has given us this name. When we hear the event that is called for in a name like "democracy," we hear an old name and an old promise, a promise first made among the Greeks, to whose language this word belongs, and we are called back to the long history of the efforts that have been made over the centuries to make this name come true. We hear the history of success, but we no less hear what the theologian Johannes Baptist Metz, following the lead of Jewish writer Walter Benjamin, called the *memoria passionis*, the memory of the suffering that has been endured in the name of democracy, in the name of the event that has been promised in that name. That is a notion that is profoundly rich in its implications for Christianity, which is organized around its own *memoria passionis*: the memory of the passion of Jesus, which Metz calls the "dangerous memories of the sufferings of Jesus."[3] Dangerous to whom? To the powers that be, to the long robes of the present order, to a world that wants to close over and close off and repress those memories of past injustice.

By the same token, it also belongs to the vocativeness of the event to be addressed, to be called on, *here and now*, in the present, to be made responsible, to be asked to respond, to what this name calls for. We are reminded of the way the congregation in Sheldon's opening scene was put on the spot by the appearance of someone who should have reminded them of Jesus, when he "called on" them in an uninvited way, and in so doing elicited from them a promise about how they would live in the future. We must be responsible to events, responsive to them, welcome them, and show them hospitality when they show up uninvited at our door. We must, as Deleuze says, make ourselves worthy of the events that befall us, worthy of the name that harbors these events—names like democracy or Christianity.[4] We are thus not only called forward and called back by the event, but we are also called on. Remember that in the theory of the event, "truth" means what is trying to come true, which points to our responsibility to make it actually come true—let us say, to give it a Pauline twist, to fill up what is missing in the body of this name (Col. 1:24). Benjamin put this point in an odd but striking way. He said that the messianic age is not off in the future but *right now*, that *now* is the messianic age, that *we* are the messianic people, we are the ones whom the dead were waiting for—to right the wrong of their sufferings.[5] That is not unlike what Abraham Lincoln said at the Gettysburg Cemetery: that we here today must resolve that these dead will not have died in vain—this "will not have," which in grammar is called the "future anterior," being of special importance in deconstruction. That is how things work in the vocative order, where memories can be dangerous and where our dreams for what is promised are also dangerous, as two of the most famous orations in American history confirm (Lincoln's and King's). They endanger the present order, challenging the pretense of the present form of things—the existential order—to pass itself off as the event itself, to actually *be* democracy or justice or truth or Christianity or whatever it pretends to "be," whatever it says it "is," whatever the "powers that be" are trying to get away with. That is why when Derrida once famously described deconstruction as a critique of the "metaphysics of presence," he took the side of the better angels of our nature, even though his detractors thought he was the devil himself. (Actually, for strategic reasons, he is better off on the "devilish" side, angels on the whole being a little too pious for deconstructors.)

Derrida sometimes describes the event by saying that while the event is possible, it represents a very special kind of "perhaps."[6] This is because it is a prayer not for what is straightforwardly possible but for "the possibility of *the* impossible." This is my favorite description of deconstruction; it is the one that Derrida himself calls its "least bad definition."[7] What is "possible" in the straightforward sense is the foreseeable future, the future that we can reasonably anticipate and plan for and that can be called the "future present." That, of course, is of the utmost importance. We can and should foresee and plan for the education of our children and for our own retirement; we should plan our calendar and our time commitments. But by *the* impossible he means something that exceeds the horizon of foreseeability and expectation and not a simple logical contradiction (like p *and* ~p). He means the possibility of something more "unconditional," which he calls the "absolute" future, the future that takes us by surprise, the one that lies beyond our horizon of expectation. That is the future of the event, like the way hope is truly hope when it has been pushed up against the impossible and everything looks hopeless.[8]

A Prayer for Justice

I am identifying deconstruction as a kind of passion or prayer for the impossible, or as an affirmation of the "undeconstructible." The first time I find mention of something "undeconstructible" is in a 1989 essay titled "The Force of Law."[9] This essay is the best place to start with the more overtly religion-friendly accenting of deconstruction in Derrida's writings.[10]

The law is always deconstructible, Derrida writes, but "justice in itself, if such a thing exists, outside or beyond law, is not deconstructible" ("Force of Law," 14). The deconstructibility of the law, Derrida adds, is not "bad news"—in fact it is a stroke of luck. As readers of St. Paul's Letter to the Romans would be able to see, this suggests a comparison with the distinction between grace and the law, a point that is worked out very nicely in a recent study of Derrida and Paul,[11] even as it suggests the attitude that Jesus had toward the law. On the one hand, the law as such only ensures legality, not justice; when the laws that are in force are unjust, we say that might makes right, that is, real injustice is cloaked with merely legal right. That is how opponents of abortion consider *Roe v. Wade*, and that is how advocates of gun control view the laws protecting gun owners. Both groups think the law lets us get away with murder. On the other hand, justice as such, without the law, is just a dream. Justice in itself is an unconditional demand, but of itself, it has no flesh and bones, no force, no teeth. Deconstruction turns on, is made possible by, and "takes place in the interval between" the undeconstructibility of justice and the deconstructibility of the law ("Force of Law," 15), between something undeconstructible but without force and something forceful but deconstructible.

In the terms I have introduced, "justice" belongs to the vocative order: it is what is called for and what calls on us, what we pray for, while laws belong to the existential order. Laws exist, but justice calls. Laws are deconstructible because laws have been constructed to begin with; laws are "positive," which means historical, regional, variable, repealable, amendable. But laws should always have the event of justice in mind. Laws may or may not be just in fact, and they may very well start out just and become unjust when the circumstances change but the laws do not. Thus there might once have been circumstances in which the personal right to bear arms was justified, although one would expect a Christian to have a very delicate conscience about such things; but to support such laws today, when the dangers to life and limb from the proliferation of such weapons is as plain as the nose on your face, defies comprehension, especially for Christians. That is why the deconstructibility of the law serves the cause of justice, which is not deconstructible. There is no better "example," if that is all it is, of why the word "deconstruction" does not signify something destructive (although it is always risky). If laws were not deconstructible they would soon become monsters that menace justice, the way the National Rifle Association menaces justice today. In Derrida's carefully crafted expression, that "justice in itself, if there is such a thing, is not deconstructible," the qualification "if there is such a thing" (*s'il y en a*) makes all the difference, a messianic difference. Justice in itself does not exist but it is something we demand and something that is demanded of us. Justice is what we call for and something that calls on us, something we solicit and something by which we are solicited, a matter of prayer and solicitation. In the deconstruction of the law, the law is exposed to the call of justice in order to provoke the reinvention of the law, thus offsetting the tendency the law has to close down around itself. Justice aerates the law, turns its soil, keeping it just.

Of a vocative like justice, we should say not "it is" but rather "it calls." Speaking of justice Derrida says in French *il y a*, just as Heidegger, speaking of Being, said in German *es gibt*, both of which get translated into English as "there is," but there is no "is" in the French or German, which is to their advantage. Justice is not a being that exists but an event that "appeals" to us, demanding our response. "There is" justice, *if* there is (*s'il y en a*). When Derrida says "if there is such a thing," he is saying not that he regards justice as a Platonic form that exists outside space and time, or as a pure utopian ideal advanced by Thomas More, but rather that it has the character of a messianic hope and demand, an open-ended appeal, a solicitation that everywhere exceeds the condition that reality itself has attained. It has a more open-ended and unforeseeable quality than a Platonic *eidos*, which is precisely an ideal we see but cannot attain. Laws exist under real and determinate circumstances, under definite conditions that vary from time to time and place to place, while the demand for justice is unconditional. Laws are real but justice is like a "ghost," a specter, that haunts the laws, a good ghost, a caring spirit or guardian angel, whispering words of justice in the ears of the law, incessantly calling for what is yet to be.

We like to say that laws are "blind"—the scales of the law are administered by a blinded figure—meaning that they are universals, applied to everyone equally, allowing no special treatment, providing "equal protection" to everyone, but binding everyone with equal force, no exceptions for the big contributors to a political campaign. But if laws are universals, justice is sensitive to the singularity of the situation, to the idiosyncrasies and differences, and it is positively mad over these little singularities. Once again, the biblical resonance is plain: laws have to do with the ninety-nine, but justice has to do with the one lost sheep, with the one lost coin, with the widow, the orphan, and the stranger. Every time we feel unjustly treated by the law we say, "But this case is different." A body of laws precise enough to cover everything singular, a perfect set of laws, would be like a map that is so exact that it is the same size as the region of which it is the map. A perfect map, a perfect set of laws, would be perfectly useless, a nightmare.

Laws have a strong existential force; there is a whole order of police, courts, and prisons to "enforce" the law. So if you break the law you stand a good chance of feeling the force of its long arm, which happened to both Paul and Jesus. But justice has only a weak or vocative force: in itself it has no institutional apparatus, no police or army, no place to lay its head; its kingdom, you might say, is not of this world. It is only a weak force. So you may very well refuse its call and get away with it; that happens all the time. Sometimes, if you have enough influence with the lawmakers, you can violate the demands of justice under the protection of the law and persecute the just; this happens all the time. The Bush administration does it every day by unjustly making the poor poorer while shrinking the size of the middle class and filling the pockets of the rich with perfectly legal tax breaks (which does not mean there are no honest people among the rich or dishonest ones among the poor). What we want, what we desire, with a desire beyond desire, is a justice with the force of law and laws that answer to the call of justice.

On this point the voice of deconstruction is not far from the voice of the prophets, which calls for justice to flow like water over the land.[12] Indeed, it is a sad commentary on the Christian Right to see how vociferously its call for "law and order" hardly makes any mention of justice. The Christian Right is all for the force of law, for rigorously enforcing laws against illegal immigrants, for keeping order in the streets, and they applaud wooden formulas like "three strikes and you're out" while slandering jurists who value discernment and adjudication as merely pandering to criminals. But it makes little mention of the biblical demands for social justice and it does little to address the injustice suffered by people who are forced to leave their homes and native lands to try to squeeze out a meager living in a foreign land. It turns a deaf ear to the poverty of inner-city life that makes a life of crime an inviting alternative to working for below-subsistence wages and no health care. They campaign vigorously for right-wing politicians who grant increasing tax breaks to the wealthy but refuse to raise the minimum wage—in the name of Jesus! The cry of the Christian Right for "law and order" drowns out the words of Deuteronomy (24:12–22), which tell the Israelites to respond to the needs of the widows and orphans and resident aliens, even as the Lord God led them out of Egypt.

Derrida condenses his view of justice into what he calls the three "aporias" of the law. In deconstruction the hermeneutical situation is always aporetic, that is, the situation in which interpretation is called for is sufficiently sharpened only when we appreciate the impossible bind or impasse in which we are caught. It is only when we realize that things are getting impossible that we start to get anywhere. As long as things are clearly "possible," we are cruising along on automatic pilot, nothing special is demanded of us, the oars are up, and we are going with the flow, hardly making any decisions at all. Nothing is happening; the "event" is not in play. Thus, the event of justice stirs within the rule of law in the following three impasses.

1. The *epoche* of the rule. The law provides a rule that must be applied to a situation, but if the rule is applied routinely and mechanically without insight into the particulars of the situation, if the law is reduced to a simple "calculation" or to producing a "programmable" result, then the law will be unjust. "Three strikes and you're out" represents the height of injustice because it prevents the judge and the jury from making a "fresh judgment" and "reinventing" the law, here and now. The truly "responsible interpretation"—responsible to the call or the demands of justice—will be both regulated (have a law) and unregulated ("suspend"—which is what *epoche* means—the law). The judge and jury must proceed under the law but they

must not be reduced to calculating machines. They must respect the difference of this situation, the justice that is called for or demanded, here and now; they must respect the event by which we are solicited in these concrete circumstances. We should never say a law as such is just or that some person as such is just, for there are too many times when each fails to respond to the demands of justice. The most we could hope for is that in this moment, here and now, the event of justice will flash, and once that occurs, it will no longer be just simply to repeat that decision in the next set of circumstances, which may be different.

2. The ghost of the undecidable. A just decision becomes a real decision only when it passes through the "undecidable," that is, through the oscillation between two conflicting decisions—when justice is making a demand on us from both sides, from two different directions—and that oscillation has to be resolved one way or the other. The most famous case of this in biblical literature is the story of the binding of Isaac, which Derrida, following Kierkegaard, has taken up.[13] That is when a decision is most responsible, most responsive to the solicitations of justice; otherwise we can beg off and say we were just following the law. From this we can see that undecidability—*pace* its vociferous critics—is the condition of possibility of a real decision, not the opposite of one. The opposite of undecidability is not decisiveness but decidability, which means programmability, derivability from a rule. Undecidability ensures that a decision will be the issue of a human "judgment," not the application of a rule, which could be done by a computer. The predecessor of undecidability in the history of ethics is not Nietzsche's theory of fictions but Aristotle's notion of practical reason (*phronesis*), which is the capacity to judge amid shifting and variable circumstances and to bring a schema to bear in an unprecedented situation; *phronesis* is the model for all hermeneutics, for which understanding is always interpretation. While in Aristotle this represents a form of practical "reason," there is also something wonderfully "mad" here—"deconstruction is mad about this kind of justice" ("Force of Law," 25)—with a kind of divinely deconstructive madness, the way one is a mad fool for the kingdom of God.

3. Urgency. Justice does not wait. However undecidable the situation may be, however much deliberation is required, however true it is that justice does not quite exist, the truth is that justice deferred is justice denied. Justice is always to come, never real-

ized, always soliciting from ahead, but at the same time justice is demanded now. At some point, the transition from deliberation to decision must be made, which inevitably takes the form of what Kierkegaard called a "leap," "acting in the night of non-knowledge and non-rule" ("Force of Law," 26). That does not mean the simple absence of knowledge and rule, thus insuring a blind and wild choice, but rather the necessity to act inventively, to make a judgment where there are no guard rails or clear precedents, literally, to de-cide, to make the cut, to respond to the event here soliciting us. We must go as far as we can with calculation, but then beyond calculation make the cut, terminate the interminable, decide the oscillation of the undecidable, make the impossible happen.

That indeed is what deconstruction "is," if it is:

> It [deconstruction] is possible as an experience of the impossible, there where, even if it does not exist (or does not yet exist, or never does exist), *there is* [*il y a*] justice. Wherever one can replace, translate, determine the x of justice, one should say: deconstruction is possible, as impossible, to the extent (there) where *there is* (undeconstructible) x, thus to the extent (there) where *there is* (the undeconstructible). ("Force of Law," 15)

In deconstruction, one sets out in search of, or rather, one is oneself searched out or called on by whatever is unconditional, or undeconstructible, in a given order, and it is precisely in virtue of this undeconstructible *x*, which does not exist, which does not exist yet, which never quite exists, that everything that does exist in that order is deconstructible. Whatever exists, whatever is present, is contingent, historical, constructed under determinate conditions—like the church or the Sabbath—and as such is inwardly disturbed by the undeconstructible, unconditional impulse that stirs within it—which for the church is the event that occurs in the name of Jesus. To "deconstruct" is on the one hand to analyze and criticize but also, on the other hand, and more importantly, to feel about for what is living and stirring within a thing, that is, feeling for the event that stirs within the deconstructible structure in order to release it, to set it free, to give it a new life, a new being, a future. Is it lawful to do good on the Sabbath? That is why deconstruction is affirmation, doubly so, *oui, oui*, the affirmation of the impossible, of the undeconstructible event whose life it bears within it like an expectant mother, which means a mother who expects and prays for an event.

The Gift

We cannot do everything "for the money," for the pay off. There have to be things we do for the sheer love of them, things that are given to us to which we in turn give ourselves, where we break the chain of means-and-ends. That is what is behind the madness that deconstruction shows for the "gift," which is one of Derrida's most well-known and characteristic discussions. The gift is a paradigm of an impossible and aporetic situation, even though it seems for all the world simple enough.[14] A gives x to B, freely and graciously. But consider the chain of consequences that is thereby set off. It is common courtesy for B to respond with gratitude, to say "thank you," for example, while also making a mental note to repay the gift, not right away, of course, which would be obvious and rude, but in a discrete and timely fashion. So the generous gesture on the part of A inevitably moves B to give y to A. Part of B's discretion, too, will be to get a sense of what x (the original gift) is worth, because it would also violate the protocol of gift giving to return the gift with something very cheap, or the opposite, to humiliate A by repaying the gift later on with something very expensive, which makes A look bad. Checking prices online is a handy and discreet way to determine the range in which to shop or at least in which to keep an eye out for something with which one might "casually" return the gift. Of course, the timing of a lot of gift exchanging is more regulated than this, as on birthdays or Christmas, but you still need to carefully gauge the value of the gifts in which you are trading.

Notice what has happened: as soon as the gift is given, the gift begins to annul itself. How so? We started with A trying to give a gift to B, but no sooner has this taken place than B is encumbered with a sense of debt that B sets about trying to discharge. Along with receiving a gift, B received a debt. We speak of "owing a debt of gratitude" to someone, and that is a fair enough description. Instead of merely being given something, B has gone into debt. In contrast, A, who ought to be experiencing a lack now that A is bereft of what A has given away, has added to his reputation for generosity. By giving x to B, A has come out ahead and B has come out behind. That is the very opposite of what A set out to do, and B immediately sets about to restore the equilibrium. The gift is supposed to be an act of "giving," but it has quickly turned into an economy, a matter of "debts" and "repayment," of balance of payments. The idea behind a gift ideally ought to be to give a gift without return, to make an expenditure without the expectation of reciprocation, in a kind of "mad" generosity. But the result is a thinly disguised economy of exchange that cooly calculates the value of the gift and is very much governed by the principle of sufficient reason. What started out as the madness of the gift, a one-way giving without return, has turned into a circle of exchange. Indeed, that is why giving "gifts" to public officials needs to be regulated—because the big-time donors expect a big-time return on their "investment," which is not just a gift. Moreover, we can all think of friends and relatives whose gift giving is intended to buy them favor and influence.

Is there no way out of this circle? Suppose A gives the gift anonymously so that B does not know whom to thank? That will only make things worse, for then B will be blocked from ever discharging this debt while A will congratulate himself for the nobility of his nature, which is such as to give an anonymous gift and not expect a show of gratitude. Or suppose I give my children the gift of an inheritance for which I will not, in principle, be around to receive expressions of gratitude. Still, I know in the quiet of my mind how profoundly grateful my children will be, and I am repaid over and over again by the prospect that they will prosper as a result of my generous benefaction. Indeed, I am sometimes given to wonder if I might not get an excellent portrait of my own good self made for them to hang in a place of prominence as a constant reminder of my boundless beneficence. Then suppose, by contrast, a situation where your gift is met with cold ingratitude—surely that would stop the circle in its tracks. Not so, for then you would congratulate yourself still more, this time for the superiority of your gift-giving nature over the mean-spiritedness of this wretched ingrate on whom you have spent your time and energy. In short, it seems that as soon as anyone is conscious that anything has been given, the circle is set in motion and the gift begins to annul itself.

From this discussion critics of Derrida, like the philosophical theologian Jean-Luc Marion, have concluded that for Derrida the self-annulling character of the gift means that the gift is impossible.[15] But that is to cut Derrida's discussion short, to applaud before the last movement has been played, or to leave at intermission, before the lecture is over, and not stay around for its conclusion. The conclusion is not that the gift is impossible but that the gift is *the* impossible (it belongs to the vocative order), which is why we love it so and why we are mad about the gift with the madness of love itself, which dreams of the impossible. The aporia, *the* impossible, is never the end of action in deconstruction but the start, the condition of possibility of a genuine action, one with teeth in it. So what Derrida actually concludes from the analysis of this aporia is twofold:

First, *know* what the gift is and how the gift works. Know that the gift sets off the circle of return and appreciate the aporetic situation— but still *give*. It is impossible that the gift will not in one way or another be reciprocated, even as it is impossible to purge ourselves of every expectation of a return, for even were such purity of intention possible for our consciousness, there would be no telling what is going on in our unconscious. But still *give*, make the Kierkegaard-ian leap, seize the madness of the moment, and give, expecting no return—even though there will inevitably be a return. Circles there always are, like the poor, but in virtue of the gift the circles are opened up. The circular economies in which we conduct our lives are thereby widened, becoming more open ended and generous, expanding into ever-wider rings of generosity and beneficence.

Second, to this first bit of advice, Derrida adds a second coun-sel: give economies a chance. Economies, after all, are all that exist, while the gift, if there even is such a thing, is *the* impossible. (Gifts belong to the vocative and poetic order, economies to the colder, less poetic order of the existential and the factual.) But economies are everywhere and all around us—in the workplace, the schools, medicine, the law, the government. Economies are how things happen, how they get done. Not many people can work just for their health (*salut*); people expect a salary (*salaire*) with benefits. But then again, consider what would happen if there were *only* economies, if nobody did anything except for a buck. Of course, teachers, lawyers, nurses, doctors, and the rest of us expect and deserve a fair wage and a decent salary; but consider what a nightmare it would be if no one did anything except for a return, if no one did anything extra, made a special effort to see that things were done well, if no one went the extra mile. That goes for employers, too—employers especially—who should not expect to exploit their workers in virtue of the deconstruction of the gift! When people on either end of a contract are reduced to working the contract, to doing nothing but what the contract literally demands, the result is a nightmare. Economies are made fertile and productive by the gift by which they are ruptured and interrupted, punctuated, opened up, and expanded. Economies need gifts even as the gift goes beyond what is needed.[16]

We might say that every existing gift, every "present" (in French *cadeau*, from the Latin *catena*, meaning "chain"), is deconstructible, which means it sets off a circle (or a chain) of exchange, but the gift in itself, if there is such a thing—in French *le don*, from *donner* (French), *donare* (Latin)—is not deconstructible. Economies are what exist but the gift calls to us from beyond the order of existence and being, soliciting us to go beyond what is, which here means to give, to make an expenditure without reserve, to go where you cannot go. The gift, *if there is such a thing*, is the event, the impossible, the undeconstructible. The gift is what we love and desire with a desire beyond desire, in which we hope with a hope against hope. The gift is given with love, even if we are not loved in return.

Derrida's analysis of the gift has several important implications for Christianity. In the first place, it constitutes a ringing warning against allowing a spiritual capitalism to invade our thinking about the kingdom, against bringing an investment mentality to the kingdom. The saints have often warned us about just such a creeping celestial capitalism, which is very likely to seep into our understanding of the counsels Jesus gives in the Synoptics. Jesus says to practice your piety in secret—to give alms in secret, to pray in secret—because otherwise you will have a reward for your piety here on earth instead of being rewarded later in heaven (Matt. 7:21–28). That would be like selling your stock short, before it reaches its full worth. In our effort to avoid hypocrisy—parading our piety in public—we must also beware of making everything turn on rewards, even long-term celestial rewards. Such piety must always take the form of the gift, if there is such a thing, which ought not to be allowed to degenerate into a bald economy. For the gift is made from love, and love, as Meister Eckhart said, is "without why." Love is its own why; love is for its own sake. It does not demand a further or external reason. When I do something for love of my spouse or child or friend, that is an expenditure made without expectation of return, even though we understand that in fact the circle of return is always there. The force of deconstruction in this context is to preserve the "madness" of the gift giving, the expenditure that is made madly on behalf of the other, and to delimit the rigorous—as in *rigor mortis*—rationality of cost accounting our lives. There is, there ought to be, something that we do in life that is not for a return but just because what we are doing is life itself, something a little mad. That is the gift.

Forgiveness

But there is another and perhaps even more poignant point of contact between deconstruction and the New Testament, and that is the question of forgiveness, to which Derrida devoted several lectures and seminars in the last decades of his life.[17] Once again, his approach was aporetic: the only thing that can be truly forgiven is the unforgivable; the only condition under which true forgiveness is possible is when forgiveness is impossible. How is that so? Forgiveness ought to be a matter of the gift, not of an economy. Is there not a graciousness, a gratuity, a giftlike character at play whenever I forgive someone or am myself forgiven? Is that not why we speak of the "grace" of forgiveness? Or is this just a fair deal? Normally the news is filled with stories of violence, rancor, and revenge, but occasionally we read in the newspapers or see on television stories of people who have forgiven someone who has murdered their child or spouse or parent, and we wonder how that is possible. It is beyond understanding, beyond reason, beyond all accounting, all cost accounting.[18] It is a gift, bearing witness to the possibility of *the* impossible. If you borrow money from the bank and then make all the payments on the loan, the bank says the debt is "forgiven"—but this is strictly bank talk. Banks do not make gifts, and when they do we know they are up to something, trying to sell us some new service they have come up with. Nor do they forgive anything. They are business people and strict in their accounting.

Now the theological traditions, both Christian and Jewish, have tended to behave like bankers when it comes to forgiveness. That is, they spell out the conditions under which forgiveness is possible, typically four in number. Forgiveness requires an expression of sorrow, the intention to make amends, a promise not to repeat the offense, and a willingness to do penance. If someone meets all four conditions then they have *earned* forgiveness. We *owe* it to them the way the bank owes us the deed once the mortgage is paid off. A deal is a deal. But a deal is not a gift, and a gift is not a deal. Then what would it mean to forgive someone? It would have to mean something uneconomic—like a gift—something unconditional, something unaccountable, something mad. But the New Testament turns on just such unaccountables—like loving your enemies. If you love those who love you, what good is that? It makes perfect sense. Even the mafia does that. The unaccountable excess of love is felt when you love your enemies, when you love the unlovable—those whom it is unreasonable to love—which is the madness of the kingdom, which follows the nonprinciple of nonsufficient reason! Just so, the unaccountable excess of forgiveness is felt when we forgive precisely those who do not meet some or all of the four conditions, who are not sorry, do not repent, and do not intend to mend their ways. That is, genuine forgiveness is offered unconditionally, not subject to meeting any or all of these four conditions, exactly the way Jesus prayed for the forgiveness of the Roman soldiers. Just so, we often speak of things that are unforgivable—the Holocaust, say, or the atrocities of American slavery or of apartheid, or the several attempts at genocide we have witnessed in the past century. But would not such unforgivable things be the very subject matter of genuine forgiveness?

E. P. Sanders, the distinguished New Testament scholar, has ventured the hypothesis that, considering how much unfavorable attention the teachings of Jesus drew down on himself, Jesus might just have taught some such unorthodox—or mad—variation on the classical doctrine of Teshuvah. Jesus, it is said, consorted with sinners; the text does not specify with former or reformed sinners, but simply says sinners. It just might be, Sanders thinks, that Jesus was making an offer of unconditional forgiveness, that he did not insist that they first repent or promise to make amends. He may very well have been teaching that in the kingdom where God reigns, they are forgiven unconditionally. Had Jesus done so, he may well have given scandal to more traditional rabbis, who saw forgiveness in terms of its classical conditions and thus who submitted forgiveness to the principle of sufficient reason.[19]

There is still another twist to the aporias of the gift and forgiveness, and perhaps even the most important twist of all. If the invisible God is revealed in the visible icon or figure of Jesus in the New Testament, and if the teachings of Jesus turned on forgiveness in an important way, then the God of Jesus is a God of forgiveness. But if forgiveness is a gift and not an economic exchange, that puts in question the classical terms in which we think of the death of Jesus, specifically as "atonement" or as a debt paid to the Father that squares our accounts with God. Is the Father the "Keeper of All Accounts"? Or is the Father not imaged best in the father portrayed in the story of the prodigal son? For if the younger son was prodigal or profligate with his inheritance, was not the father in turn prodigal or prodigious in his love? When the son returned home, this father did not seek to determine the right measure of punishment that would redress the offense and repair his wounded dignity. He did not look to settle the accounts, but rather set aside all such calculation for the excess of love he bore his son! So he threw a party that bent the nose of the older son out of joint; the father looked weak to the older son, whose resentment made him look bad. Is not the highly Anselmian story we have been telling ourselves in atonement theology completely at odds with the figure of the father in this parable told by Jesus? Is not the God of Jesus marked first and foremost by forgiveness? Are the dealings of the Father with the world governed by the principles of economics, of exchanging this for that, or by the nonprinciples, the uneconomics, of love?

Hospitality

There is another point that I have yet to mention in which the excess of the gift in deconstruction makes contact with the text of the New Testament, and that is the attention that Derrida gave to "hospitality" in his later lectures and seminars. Hospitality is another of those words that resonate with the event—words that promise something that they do not quite deliver—representing another case of the "madness" of the messianic.[20] Once again, it all starts out very innocently. What hospitality means seems simple enough: welcoming the other, welcoming the coming of the other into the same, into my house, for example. But when in fact we actually offer hospitality, whom do we typically invite? Our friends, of course, those whose company we enjoy and from whom we can expect reciprocity

(the circle of exchange), or else people whose favor we are curry-
ing. Either way, we welcome only those who serve our pleasure or
our interests, which means tightening the circle of the same, not
welcoming the other. One very good proof of this is that we depend
on the discretion of those whom we invite not to broadcast it all
over creation, lest others—the real others, in this case—discover
that they were not invited. So there is a good deal of inhospitality
built into our hospitality. We welcome those who are welcome to
begin with, not those who are unwelcome. But if hospitality is what
we say it is—that is, welcoming the other—then ought it not be a
matter of welcoming those who are unwelcome? Should it not be
extended beyond our neighbors to strangers? Beyond our friends
to our enemies? Beyond the invited to the uninvited? In fact, is not
the very act of invitation foreign to the idea of hospitality—genuine
or unconditional hospitality—inasmuch as "inviting" is a selection
process whereby one puts in place in advance a set of prior conditions under which the hospitality will be exercised? Would not the
most radical or unconditional hospitality be a hospitality without
invitation, a welcoming of the uninvited? Derrida insists on distinguishing between invitation and visitation: hospitality by invitation
is always conditional, a compromised and programmed operation,
as opposed to hospitality to the uninvited other—who pays us an
unexpected visit—which is unconditional and unprogrammed.[21]

But what is to say that I will not be murdered in my bed by all
this hospitality? How am I to distinguish between the guest and
an outright enemy, who will do me and mine the worst violence?
Am I not duty bound to protect myself and my family from such
violence? Is this messianic madness not just madness plain and
simple? Derrida's answer to these questions, which are valid questions, is that there would never be any way in principle to eliminate all the risk and still preserve the idea of hospitality.[22] There
is even a trace of this undecidability in language itself. The word
"hospitality" derives from *hostis* + *posse*. The word means, first,
to have a certain "power" (*posse*) of disposition over the place of
welcome: I cannot invite a guest to stay in someone else's home.
So it means to make my home your home, remembering that it is
my home, not yours, which is a crucial part of its tension. Second,
"hospitality" means to welcome or admit the "*hostis*," which in
Latin means the stranger, who is the guest (of a "host" in a "hotel");
but a *hostis* is sometimes the stranger who is alien or "hostile."

This very undecidability between friend or enemy is built into the language of hospitality, which leads Derrida to speak of "hosti-pitality." While Derrida is not encouraging reckless behavior, he is saying that the only way to eliminate the risk built into hospitality is to eliminate hospitality itself by screening the guests so carefully in advance that every trace of welcoming the other has been extinguished. There is always a risk in everything worthwhile. We are always put at risk whenever we welcome someone, just as we are put at risk whenever we love or trust or believe in someone, and the greater the love or hospitality, the greater the risk.

That means that there is always something slightly mad about hospitality, as indeed there is about the gift in all its forms, for what are forgiveness and hospitality if not versions of the gift, of an expenditure without return? But where indeed would one ever expect to find anything so mad? One suggestion I have is the New Testament, in which Jesus said: "When you give a luncheon or a dinner, do not invite your friends or your brothers or your relatives or rich neighbors, in case they may invite you in return, and you would be repaid. But when you give a banquet, invite the poor, the crippled, the lame, and the blind" (Luke 14:12–13).[23] This is followed by the story of the great banquet in which the invited guests make their excuses and fail to show up. Then the offended master rounds up his slaves and instructs them, "Go out at once into the streets and lanes of the town and bring in the poor, the crippled, the blind, and the lame." When told by the slaves that there is still room remaining at his tables, the master tells the slaves to round up even casual passers-by and compel them to come in (Luke 14:15–24). In Matthew, the same parable is told except there the feast is a wedding (Matt. 22:1–14), which would surely make for one of the most extraordinary wedding receptions on record! These are parties as mad as any Hatter's party dreamed up by Lewis Carroll, mad with the madness of the kingdom of God—and the madness of the gift in deconstruction.

That indeed is what is so interesting about the opening scene of Charles Sheldon's *In His Steps*, which very precisely portrays the demands of the madness of hospitality in Derrida's sense. The appearance of Jack Manning, the other one who comes knocking on the doors of the good parishioners of the First Church of Raymond, is a clear case of a visitation that is not an invitation. His appearance calls for welcoming the unwelcomed and receiving the uninvited, who show up at our door dressed in rags. We constantly pray and call for Jesus to come, but the question is—and this, we recall, is part of Derrida's analysis of the messianic—do we *really want* him to come, or is his true appearance always really *uninvited*? Is not Jesus showing up the last thing we really want to have—dressed in rags and laying claim to us in all his neediness, as one of the least among us? Or looking in at what we in the church are doing in his name? Rev. Maxwell's decision that the very essence of Christian life means the madness of turning one's life upside down in response to this visitation bears the mark, down even to the details, of what Derrida calls the messianic madness of hospitality. Christianity would be well advised to consider itself under the permanent promise/threat of just such a *visitation*—quite uninvited—by Jesus, who may at any time show up at the doors of our churches, requiring of us an accounting of what we have made of his memory or asking for a cup of cold water—or perhaps an increase in the minimum wage and basic health insurance.

Love

All along, whether we have been talking about justice or the gift, forgiveness or hospitality, the topic will have been love. Derrida once said, "Deconstruction . . . is not negative, even though it has often been interpreted as such despite all sorts of warnings. For me, it always accompanies an affirmative exigency, I would even say that it never proceeds without love."[24] Deconstruction does not take a single step without love; it always follows "in the steps" of love, following love's call. What does it love? The impossible, the undeconstructible, what is coming, the event. Deconstruction is affirmation, the affirmation of the impossible, of the coming of the event. That is what I called in the preceding chapter the "real beyond the real," the hyper-real, which participates in the structure of the step/not beyond. Every time a "deconstructive critique" is undertaken, every time something is criticized as a fiction or an unjustifiable assumption, such critiques "are always advanced *in the name of the real*, of the irreducible reality of the real, not of the real as the objective, present, perceptible or intelligible *thing (res)*, but of the real as the coming or the event of the other." But what, then, is the "real"? "The real is this non-negative im-possible, this im-possible coming or invention of the event whose thought is not an onto-phenomenology. It is a thought of the event (singularity of the other, in its unanticipatible coming, *hic et nunc*)."[25]

That is a particularly Parisian way of putting the following perfectly clear point. The "real" is precisely what eludes or withdraws from us whenever we think we have gotten it in our grips, whenever we imagine we see it (phenomenology) or can claim "there it is" (ontology) or think we can anticipate it (hermeneutic fore-structures). It is the element, the event, *in* experience that makes experience possible—because when we run into what is real, something is really happening—precisely by never being itself directly experienced. The "real" is the ultrareal in every *res*, the thing that slips away, the secret that will not yield to our advances or embrace, like an elusive lover whose play only deepens our desire. The real is what we are trying to make come true, even while it resists our comprehension, our grasp or grip: "Nothing is more 'realist,' in this sense, than a deconstruction. It is *ce qui arrive* (he who/that which arrives or happens)."[26]

What is more real, more nonsubjective, than that which resists the very grasp of the subject? Deconstruction is not realism, not because it is in love with illusion, but because it desires what is more than the real rather than settling for what is less, for the real is always deconstructible. What do we desire more than that which withdraws, that which is always already withdrawn and whose approach is always coming, always already coming, that which is never present but always drawing us on, drawing us out by withdrawing itself, soliciting and inviting us, luring us? That is what we love and pray for.

Then what is love (an ancient and venerable question!) and why does Derrida dare the formulation that deconstruction never proceeds without love? Is this not a little too edifying for a tough character like Derrida? Is his talk of love a sign that Derrida is getting soft? Is this deconstruction in its dotage? Not one bit. Remember what Jacques Lacan (who, to my knowledge, has never been accused of being too soft or smarmy) says: *les non-dupes errent*.[27] Those who think that they are too smart and too sophisticated to talk about love are just the ones to be misled. Or keep in mind Kierkegaard quoting St. Paul: love believes all things but love is not deceived! So let us hear Derrida out and not leave at intermission. On his accounting, the thing itself always slips away, which is what he, following Levinas, calls the "wholly other" that we love, what we want, in fact, to protect and "keep safe." In a manner that reminds us of nothing so much as "negative theology," he says that the thing itself is safe (*sauf*) if, and only if, it is safely secreted away, if what presents itself *as* the real is everything save (*sauf*) the thing itself, which safely slips away. That is what Levinas means when he says that love "is a relation with that which always slips away" (*une relation avec ce qui dérobe à jamais*).[28] For Derrida, in much the same sense as Levinas, love means to "surrender to the impossible," *se rendre*, to render oneself over to, to give up one's arms, and give oneself back to the impossible: "To surrender to the other, and this is the impossible, would amount to giving oneself over in going toward the other, to coming toward the other but without crossing the threshold, and to respecting, to loving even the invisibility that keeps the other inaccessible."[29] The "(loved) other," *l'autre (aimé)* must remain other, must be kept safe as other, and we must lay down our arms (*rendre les armes*) and surrender. By sacrificing or giving up the assault of "realism" on the world, we allow the thing itself to slip away—just to keep it safe and to show it our love—which is, of course, very close to Augustine saying that if you understand it, then what you understand is not God. If it is God, it eludes your grasp and always slips away.

—ᴍᴥ—

It is, of course, not enough to keep hanging one award after another on deconstruction's wall—awards for justice, the gift, forgiveness, hospitality, and even love itself—for the question will always remain: what would love or justice or hospitality require, here and now, in the concrete? While insisting there will never be criteria that will enable us to program or "derive" an answer to this question, we have at least prepared the ground for getting down to cases by first getting a sense of what deconstruction is up to, by getting a feel for its spirit, which I have characterized as a spirit of prayers and tears, of madness and excess, for justice and the gift, and which on numerous issues presents a striking contemporary counterpart to the madness of the kingdom of God and therefore does excellent service as its hermeneut. But before finally posing the question, "What would Jesus deconstruct?" as to its particulars, we have one more duty, which is to pause over the "Jesus" in this question and pursue the particular weight this name bears.

4

Jesus, the Theo-Poetics of the Kingdom, and Praxis

Suppose we alter the intonation of this question and ask, "What would *Jesus* deconstruct?" What is the uniquely Jesus-inspired thing to do? I do not mean some universal-rational thing (as if there were one!) that we might get from Socrates or Kant, but the specific genius, the divine madness that characterizes Jesus in particular. What is the characteristic mark of this "poetics" or "theo-poetics" of the kingdom that we find in the New Testament of which Jesus is the centerpiece? Then, if we can get a sense of that, let us ask how we get from any such theo-poetics to a praxis of the kingdom. How do we go from poetics to ethics and politics?

The Theo-Poetics of the Power of Powerlessness

While other cases of "divine men" are to be found in ancient literature, Jesus is unique precisely because Jesus is not a typical superhero or mythological power who slays things and crushes his enemies with his might. What is most riveting about Jesus is that he is defeated, executed, and abandoned, that he is a man whose symbol is an instrument of public execution, like a gallows, and whose message is radical peace and nonviolence.

When he is arrested he tells the disciple who wields a sword in his defense to sheathe it, for that is not how things are done in the kingdom of God (Matt. 26:52). After this the disciples desert him. As he hangs on the cross he asks forgiveness for those who are executing him. To feel the sharp edge of this scene, let us impress on ourselves that he is nailed to the cross, unable to move, unable to escape, and forget the magical images of him—that all he had to do was blink and those Roman soldiers would have been sent hurling through the air and smashed against a rock. Forget the opinion of Thomas Aquinas that Jesus was intimately conjoined with the beatific vision at that moment, which would have offered him infinite relief from suffering. I regard all that as so much docetism.

If we forget all that and think of a Jesus who really is crucified and who really feels abandoned, then the icon of God we find in Jesus on the cross is not an icon of power but of powerlessness, or at most of a power of powerlessness. Saint Paul called this the "weakness of God" (1 Cor. 1:25), which is perhaps the ultimate madness of the kingdom of God. In Jesus there is *kenosis* (Phil. 2:5–8): the divinity lies in the emptying of divinity. There is an ancient Christian tradition of being fools for God, like Simeon Stylites atop his pillar—men and women whose lives make no sense from the viewpoint of what the world calls wisdom, people sent as lambs among wolves—that goes back to Jesus. What is specific to Jesus is what Paul called the logic of the cross (*logos staurou*), which is more precisely the foolishness (*moria*) of the cross.

What rises up in majesty from the cross is not a show of might but rather forgiveness, not power but a protest against the unjust execution of a just man, a great prophetic "no" to injustice and persecution, a prophetic death rather than a sacrificial exchange that buys a celestial reward. Something unconditional lays claim to us in that weakness—something unconditional but without an exercise of force.[1] He is tried, convicted, tortured, and paraded through the streets in shame on the way to a particularly gruesome public execution, although a common enough display of imperial power in the Roman world. My God, my God, why have you deserted me? The apostles scatter; a few women keep watch. This is the original ending of Mark's Gospel, at 16:8. To catch the sense of the life and death of Jesus, my advice is to linger in that moment—on Holy Saturday—and not to rush too quickly to Easter Sunday triumphalism.

But the weakness of God has nothing to do with a timid and fearful man and everything to do with the courage of prophetic impatience. The God of forgiveness, mercy, and compassion shines like a white light on the hypocrisy of those who, under the cover of God, oppress the most defenseless people in society. I imagine that Jesus had a sharp tongue and a biting wit and did not suffer hypocrites gladly. He kept one thing uppermost in his heart, the love of neighbor and of God, which was unconditional, the sum and substance of the Torah, and he treated everything else, however sacred it was in men's eyes, as man made, conditional, flexible, deconstructible. His periodic flashes of anger are reserved for those who confused the latter with the former. He shows a preferential concern for the poor and impatience with the hypocrisy of the rich and powerful. He was himself born in poverty, and his family belonged to the lowest stratum of ancient society. When he announced his ministry he said it was directed to bringing good news to the poor, to healing the lepers and the lame, systematically giving the outcasts and the outsiders pride of place (which in deconstruction is called "strategic reversal"). His counsel to pray for our "daily bread" was meant for people living at the level of bare subsistence. He did not endorse sin, but he saw sin as an occasion for mercy and for forgiveness of the sinner, and he reserved a special anger for the hypocrisy of religious authorities who made a living denouncing sin while concealing their own corruption. The current sexual abuse of children in the church and the subsequent cover up, all in his name, are a perfect example of what sent him over the edge. When the woman is taken in adultery, he does not endorse adultery but his emphasis falls on showing mercy to the woman while coolly exposing the hypocrisy of her accusers. He prevents a barbarous stoning—if you have read Khaled Hosseini's *The Kite Runner*, you may recall from his account how sadistic a thing a stoning is—and commends her to the forgiveness of God. He did not hesitate to call a spade a spade and that finally cost him his life. His language against the religious authorities of the day (long robes who devour the houses of widows, Luke 20:47) and against the money changers in the temple (a den of thieves, Mark 11:17) was especially sharp. But he took his physical anger

out on fig trees and the money-changers' tables, not on human
bodies.

A great deal of what he has to say is condensed into the Sermon
on the Mount (Matt. 5:1–7:29), which sketches the dynamics of the
kingdom in a series of astonishing reversals of worldly wisdom. If
you are poor and hungry, then the kingdom of God is yours in a
special way; but if you are rich and full, woe to you. One paragraph
in particular, in the Lukan version, almost blisters off the page:

> But I say to you that listen, Love your enemies, do good to those
> who hate you, bless those who curse you, pray for those who abuse
> you. If anyone strikes you on the cheek, offer the other also; and
> from anyone who takes away your coat do not withhold even your
> shirt. Give to everyone who begs from you; and if anyone takes
> away your goods, do not ask for them again. Do to others as you
> would have them do to you. (Luke 6:27–31)

In short, whenever one would expect an exercise of power from
a classical hero, Jesus displays the stunning power of powerlessness—of nonviolence, nonresistance, forgiveness, mercy, compassion, generosity. The divinity that shows through Jesus consists
not in a demonstration of might but in a complete reversal of our
expectations culminating in the most stunning reversal of all. It
is the centerpiece of all this madness, the one that makes as little
sense as possible from the point of view of worldly common sense,
the most divine madness of all: love your enemies. The key to the
kingdom is to love those who do not love you, who hate you, and
whom you, by worldly standards, should also hate. That is exactly
the madness that a deconstructive analysis of love would predict.
Loving the lovable is entirely possible, but loving the unlovable,
those who are impossible to love, that is when the kingdom reigns.
Loving the unlovable, the possibility of the impossible, that is the
central symmetry that leads me to treat deconstruction as the
hermeneutics of the kingdom of God.

On those occasions in the New Testament narratives when Jesus
puts on a display of power it is not to save himself or crush his
enemies, but it is on behalf of others, by using his power of healing. He came teaching *and healing*, Mark says. He is consistently,
relentlessly concerned about the bodily needs of everyone he meets
who is down and out and in need of help. And what bodies they

are! A veritable Foucauldian parade—lame and leprous bodies, possessed and impoverished bodies, blind and starving bodies, and even a few dead bodies, a long list of outcasts and outsiders, of everyone who is, one way or another, out of power or out of luck, "on the outs." When he meets the centurion's servant, who is close to death, Jesus heals him. When he comes upon the funeral of the widow's son at Nain, he raises him, as he also raised Jairus's daughter and Lazarus, the brother of Mary and Martha. When he encounters someone possessed by a demon, he drives out the demon. When told of the hunger of the crowd of five thousand who are gathered to hear him, he feeds them. When he meets the lame, he straightens their limbs; when he comes upon a blind man, he spits in the dirt and rubs the muddy result in the blind man's eyes. His parables make the same point. When a man falls among thieves it is the Samaritan, not the priest or the Levite, in whom the kingdom of God reigns. When he instructed the disciples about how to pray, he taught them to pray to be forgiven and in turn to be forgiving and also, *pace* the Grand Inquisitor, to pray for bread.

He endures all things in his own body but will tolerate no suffering in the bodies of others; he suffers his own passion but rises up in compassion for the suffering of others. Forgiveness and bread, healing hearts and healing bodies, turning all things around in a profound and sweeping *metanoia*, a generalized metanoetics, which means to be of a new mind, a new heart, a new creation, a new order of both spirit and flesh. To announce the kingdom of God is to bring good news to all those who are poor in spirit and just plain poor, to those who hunger for justice and who are just plain hungry, to those whose minds are blinded by sin and who are just plain blind, to those whose hearts are bent by evil and whose bodies are just plain bent.

The Greek philosophers, and Aristotle in particular, pursued an idea of moderation, of finding the sensible median point and avoiding excess. But that does not give us a good fix on the figure of Jesus, whose life and death are marked precisely by excess, not the excess of violence but the excess of the gift, of finding the point of equilibrium and then recommending the step beyond so that to follow in his steps is to be committed to taking an extra step, to going the extra mile. You have heard it said, love your friends and hate your enemies, but I say love your enemies; you have heard it said, do not commit adultery, but I say if a man even lusts in his heart for a woman he has already committed adultery. He is guided not by the philosopher's "principle of sufficient reason," nor by any Greek idea of the rational mean, but by the excess of the gift, the excess of love, which is "without why," as Meister Eckhart said.[2] The opposite of love is not hate—I would have you hot or cold—but to be mean spirited, nit picking, parsimonious, never straying from inside the safe borders of an economy or a set of rules, never taking the risk of excess. The only measure of love is love without measure. Love is not measured by a rule, but rather love expends itself without return on behalf of the other. Love will stop at nothing, which is the excess that is ingredient in love. This explains why love can lead to violence, culminating in the ultimate contradiction of Christians doing violence to those who do not love Jesus, who taught us to love those who do not love us.

All this presented in a series of astonishing narratives, parables, and paradoxes, a series of reversals that make up what I am calling the "poetics of the kingdom," a theo-poetics that makes the topsy-turvy world of *Alice in Wonderland* look orderly by comparison, like that wedding feast that is much madder than the Hatter's party. If Gilles Deleuze was in search of an "event" that throws the world into a chaosmic and creative disorder, he missed a big opportunity when he neglected the New Testament. There is something wonderfully mad and anarchic, something parabolic and hyperbolic, about deconstruction, an unmistakable madness there for justice and the gift centered on the affirmation of the possibility of *the* impossible. That constitutes a postmodern philosophical or hermeneutical counterpart to the order, or disorder, or chaosmic order, found in the New Testament, which is centered around the body and the figure of Jesus and which is what I have described as a "sacred anarchy."[3] As there is something biblical in deconstruction—some of the same biblical and prophetic madness for the event of justice and of the gift—so there is something deconstructive about the New Testament, where the same madness for the impossible and love of paradox scrambles the laws of worldly common sense and submits them to the foolishness of the cross.

What is unique about Jesus? My guess is that when from time to time we meet people in whom the figure of Jesus is imaged, we might find ourselves ridiculing them as weak or mad or foolish, as indeed they are—in a very precise sense.

From a Poetics to a Politics of the Kingdom

But how are we to get from a theo-poetics of the impossible to a politics of the possible? Are we left marooned on an island of *the* impossible? There is no "derivation," no straight line, from the poetics or theo-poetics of the kingdom to any concrete political structure or public policy, but that does not mean there is no line or connection at all. Rather we are called to imagine the kingdom of God in the concrete political structures of the day, and that requires political imagination and judgment. The kingdom provides a *politica negativa*, a critical voice rather like the voice of a prophet against the king, like Amos railing against Jeroboam, calling for the invention of justice, which in turn requires, in addition to prophets, the hard work of concrete political invention, the cleverness of inventive political structures.

What would a political order look like were the poetics of the kingdom able to be transformed into a political structure? What would it be like if there really were a politics of the bodies of flesh that proliferate in the New Testament, a politics of mercy and compassion, of lifting up the weakest and most defenseless people at home, a politics of welcoming the stranger and of loving one's enemies abroad? What would it be like were there a politics of and for the children, who are the future; a politics not of sovereignty, of top-down power, but a politics that builds from the bottom up, where *ta me onta* (1 Cor. 1:28) enjoy pride of place and a special privilege? What would a political order look like if the last were first, if everything turned on lifting up the lowliest instead of letting relief trickle down from the top? What would it look like if there were a politics of loving one's enemies, not of war, let alone, God forbid, of preemptive war?

Would it not be in almost every respect the opposite of the politics that presently passes itself off under the name of Jesus? Would it not mean to make everything turn on peace not war, forgiveness not retribution, on loving one's enemies not preemptive war, on all the paradoxes and reversals that can be summarized under the name of "kingdom"? Are not the figures who publicly parade their love of power and their fear of the other under the name of Jesus singled out in advance by Jesus under the name of the whitened sepulchers and long robes whose fathers killed the prophets?

A politics of the kingdom would be marked by madness of forgiveness, generosity, mercy, and hospitality. The dangerous memory of the crucified body of Jesus poses a threat to a world organized around the disastrous concept of power, something that is reflected today in the widespread critique of the concept of "sovereignty"—of the sovereignty of autonomous subjects and the sovereignty of nations powerful enough to get away with acting unilaterally and in their own self-interests. The crucified body of Jesus proposes not that we keep theology out of politics but that we think theology otherwise, by way of another paradigm, another theology, requiring us to think of God otherwise, as a power of powerlessness, as opposed to the theology of omnipotence that underlies sovereignty.[4] The call that issues from the crucified body of Jesus solicits our response, for it is *we* who have mountains to move by our faith and *we* who have enemies to move by our love. It is *we* who have to make the weakness of God stronger than the power of the world.[5]

What Would Jesus Deconstruct?

Or, Whatever Happened to the Sermon on the Mount?

The task that remains can be staged as a scene of radical hospitality. Imagine an unexpected visitation—as opposed to an invitation—in which Jesus pays a surprise visit to the church and wants to see the books! Imagine another one of those scenarios in which Jesus appears, wholly uninvited, not in fifteenth-century Seville or turn-of-the-century Topeka, but today. Imagine him suddenly showing up, say, in the middle of an American political campaign or in an affluent American shopping mall (preferably at the height of the "Christmas" shopping season, which would certainly get his attention) or maybe even at an annual meeting of the American Academy of Religion (where, unless he was prepared to use his power to pass through walls, he would still need a badge to get into the book display) or even on the Oprah Winfrey show. Why not? Have we not described religious people as the ones who dream of things that have never been and ask, "Why not?"

All this in order to get down to cases about what Jesus would deconstruct. We have just proposed what is distinctive about

"Jesus" in this question, analyzed the "deconstruct," and pointed out the hermeneutic force of the "would." Now it is time to ask just *what* Jesus would deconstruct, to say more exactly what is what. To this end I will address in turn several concrete issues that face the church today—the questions of economic justice, militarism, patriarchy, and finally abortion and homosexuality.

In short, it is time to let a few theological feathers fly.

Jesus in Alabama

Let us begin with a visit to Alabama, starting with an episode from contemporary politics that poses my question in the concrete. Imagine Jesus showing up, uninvited—remember, as often as we say "come" he is always uninvited—about two thousand years after his birth, in 2003. That was the year Bob Riley, the governor of Alabama, was born again—from my point of view—although it nearly killed his political career. Governor Riley wanted (in effect) to make that year what the Bible calls a year of the Lord's favor on the poor. A long-time fiscal and social conservative, Riley abruptly reached the conclusion that the political and social priorities of the Alabama Republican party did not reflect the New Testament, which shows a preferential option for the poor and a special affirmation of children. The poorest children in his state attend one of the nation's most poorly funded public school systems—effectively one of the few ways out of ignorance, poverty, and crime for most black children—while wealthier and mostly white children go to private schools. So Riley proposed Amendment One, an aggressive revision of a regressive tax system that would have raised the money needed to begin repairing Alabama schools by requiring the wealthiest Alabamans to cough up their fair share. This turnabout was risky business for Riley, but he thought he had the New Testament on his side, where this is known as *metanoia*, being of a new heart, the madness of and for the kingdom of God (which has a counterpart in Paris, where it goes under the name of the madness of the gift, of the impossible). The occasion of Riley's reversal was a book by an Alabama law professor—Susan Pace Hamill, *The Least of These: Fair Taxes and the Moral Duty of Christians*[1]—who pointed out that the poorest people in Alabama pay about 11 percent of their income in state taxes while the richest get off with about 4 percent. Hamill was addressing the very thing the biblical year of the Jubilee had singled out: after fifty years the poor fall so far afield of the mainstream that they need to be worked back in.

I am not saying that Amendment One cannot stand on its own two feet, that it did not *also* make perfect long-range fiscal sense. For, quite apart from Jesus, or morality, or simple fairness, there is no good economic reason to consign a large portion of the population to unproductive lives of poverty and crime. My basic hermeneutic formula is this: if you want to draw your vision and inspiration from the New Testament, bless your heart, but you need, in addition to a good reading of the text, an independently good argument.

It is a sign of a beneficent swing of the Spirit that Riley drew wide support from the churches, including the Christian Coalition of America. Nonetheless, Amendment One was attacked, distorted, and defeated (68 percent of the voters opposed it) with considerable help from the Christian Coalition of Alabama. The Jubilee was called off, with much jubilation among the Christians in the 4 percent bracket! The poorest and most defenseless children in the state were defeated with the energetic help of the Christian Coalition, which felt called by the Spirit to answer the call of the richest, lest they have to pay their fair share, perhaps confusing profits with prophets.[2] The Left, ever vigilant bearers of the Enlightenment, who can be counted on to have a tin ear for religion and the centrality of religious meaning in daily life, was troubled by the religious rhetoric in Riley's proposal. As Jim Wallis says at the end of his wonderfully prophetic book, "The Secular Left will give up its hostility to religion and spirituality, or it will die," a lesson that may finally have sunk in during the 2006 midterm elections.[3]

Riley's story is not a typical one—American politicians are largely too spineless, too worried about reelection, and too terrified of their financial backers to do anything that bold—but it is an instructive one. Surely, our Alabama Christian brothers and sisters have noticed that Jesus specifically singles out children as embodying the kingdom, and surely they admit that we are repeatedly called to help the poor. Surely they have noticed a trend in the teachings of Jesus in the New Testament—it really does keep coming up![4]—not to mention the prophets in the Jewish Scriptures, which was the very point that Sheldon was emphasizing by asking "What would Jesus do?" in *In His Steps*:

> "Blessed are you who are poor, for yours is the kingdom of God." (Luke 6:20)

> "But woe to you who are rich, for you have received your consolation." (Luke 6:24)

(You may remember, if I may butt in, that this is described in deconstruction as the "strategic reversal" of poor over rich.)

> "The Spirit of the Lord is upon me, because he has anointed me to bring good news to the poor. He has sent me to proclaim release to the captives and recovery of sight to the blind, to let the oppressed go free, to proclaim the year of the Lord's favor." (Luke 4:18)

The year of the Lord's favor is the Jubilee year, the fiftieth year, a "sabbatical of sabbaticals" (the year after seven-times-seven years), in which all debts are released and land redistributed more equitably. That idea, which, if he had thought of it, Derrida might have called "the year of the gift," is not to my knowledge found in Adam Smith or John Locke, but it has unassailable scriptural credentials. Even if you spend most of your time going over your stock portfolio, it is hard to miss both the letter and the spirit behind this sort of thing in the Jewish and Christian Scriptures. But the Christian Coalition of Alabama thinks gifts are a private matter and any such counsel is the duty of private charity, not the government. They even think that in this high-tech information age public education is a gift, not a public responsibility.[5] At this point they suddenly become eloquent in defense of keeping the church and state separate. This fine constitutional point seems to slip their mind on other occasions, like their resistance to removing Chief Justice Roy Moore's monument to the Ten Commandments from the judicial building in Montgomery. To this we might also add the irony of the evidence gathered by Ronald Sider in *The Scandal of the Evangelical Conscience* and other works that shows that as evangelicals have become more upwardly mobile their charitable giving has decreased, which is not exactly the sort of reversal recommended by the New Testament.[6] Can we see the figure of Jesus here? Is this what he meant? Is this how he would translate his spirit into action today? Or do we find him weeping, not only over Jerusalem, over which he would be weeping today more than ever, but over the long robes who devour the houses of widows under the name of contemporary Christianity?

I may be forgiven (I depend a lot on that Christian virtue) if I have concluded that the private-charity argument is a cynical cover for greed, which has a way of working things out so that I get to keep as much money as I can for myself and let the poorest of the poor go to the devil. I have the idea that this is precisely the sort of hypocrisy that made Jesus flash with anger, so that if Jesus showed up one day uninvited and caught me holding forth on that point, the "revelation" I would experience would be of his meaner side. The more Jesus-inspired thing to do today, in my opinion, is to translate the gospel's commitment to the poor into an effective public policy that would actually implement an evangelical imperative, to come to the aid of the weakest and most defenseless people in society, above all the children. On this point, it is not (only) the government that has its hands in my pockets, but Jesus, and rightly so. If Jesus ever said, "My money is mine, I worked hard for it and I want to keep it for myself and there are other things that I would rather spend it on than those Samaritans," we have lost the manuscript. For "Samaritans," read poor and black! One can say this is not a white-and-black issue, but the plausibility of that claim is right up (or down) there with a six-thousand-year-old world.

Indeed, I would imagine that if the New Testament is our *literal* guide, then the standard tax rate for Christians should be set at 100 percent. The early Christians lived in common and distributed to one another according to their needs; in fact, one of the first disputes to break out in the church was whether this distribution was truly equal (Acts 6:1). I am still looking for the text that supports the idea that "Christians" means people who should be free to accumulate as much wealth for themselves as they possibly can under the law while letting the needs of the poor be met painlessly by "charity"—by people of means who will voluntarily give of their overflow—so that they do not have to share any more of their wealth than is unavoidable. In the course of looking for that text I found the story of the widow who gives two pence to the poor, whom Jesus prefers to the rich, who can afford to give of their abundance (Luke 21:1–4). What Jesus expressly commends is that the widow gives out of her very substance (*ousia*) and not out of her overflow, a point that, in the language of deconstruction, does not seem to have "arrived" in 68 percent of Alabama. She is not giving "charity," she is giving her blood. As Derrida says, she gives what she does not have to give—that is the gift, the impossible.[7] I would bring all this up at the next meeting of the Christian Coalition of Alabama and point out that it makes me nervous that greed cloaking itself under the name of God is precisely the sort of hypocrisy that particularly provoked the wrath of Jesus; I would also recommend a reading of Jacques Derrida on the gift.

While I think that all this is as close to the plain sense of the Scriptures as one is likely to find there, I repeat that I do not think that it can be nailed down by Bible thumping. (For one thing, quoting the New Testament may turn the secular Left against the poor by concluding that if the Bible is for the poor, it is against them.) That is why we need hermeneutics. One can quote the New Testament to many ends, so one always needs a good argument to go along with a good reading. To paraphrase Dale Martin, to hear what the Bible says, set it carefully on your desk and listen quietly. After a long enough silence has passed it may hit you that it does not talk; you have to read and interpret it.[8]

I have all along been speaking of the "poetics of the kingdom," or the "theo-poetics of Jesus,"[9] and I have avoided speaking of "the politics of Jesus," an expression that I think is inherently ambiguous and too easy to abuse. It can be invoked by everyone from John Howard Yoder, who is a pacifist, to George W. Bush, who used it to launch a preemptive war against Iraq. There is every good reason to believe that Jesus did not act or regard himself as a political thinker or reformer and that he regarded the kingdom of God as a word spoken to the Jews that asked them to be of a new heart and to prepare for God's coming. In the meantime, he asked the Jews to "render to Caesar the things that are Caesar's and to God the things that are God's." That was a snappy thing to say, which probably meant, go figure it out for yourself. But Jesus was too much a pure prophetic voice of protest against the compromises of the world to fit inside a particular political frame. He was too much a poetic voice for the impossible to be translated easily into a particular political order, which is inevitably the art of the possible. As Richard Holloway says, Jesus belongs to a "cleansing minority . . . who refuse to play the power game," and he worked "outside society's formal structures."[10] In the language of deconstruction, he worked on the borders, on the inside/outside.

Jesus himself seems to imply that the world and the kingdom of God run on separate tracks until the day God breaks in and asserts his rule over the powers of this world.[11] You might then go on to use that reading—which is fair enough as far as it goes—as a basis for saying that your duties today as a Christian have to do with your private life and public policy is a different thing, and that while you should try to do the right thing as a citizen you ought not to drag your Christianity into the picture.[12] You might even conclude, the New Testament clutched closely to your breast, that keeping your money in your pocket and letting the poor fend for themselves with whatever private charity happens to "arrive" their way is your way of serving the wretched of the earth and responding to the "good news." If, in addition, you do not rent pornographic DVDs and you refrain from drinking wine, the odds are that heaven will be yours. So nothing is settled by identifying what Jesus did in the New Testament and then trying to literally reproduce it today. One exegesis of the "Caesar saying" would suggest we let the poor rot unless and until they get lucky, which is still the prevailing view among a good many Christians today of what "bringing good news to the poor" means. In the year of the Jubilee, the rich get richer and celebrate another tax break.[13] The question is, how good a reading is that?

That is why we require hermeneutics. It is *our responsibility* to breathe with the spirit of Jesus, to implement, to invent, to convert this poetics into a praxis, which means to make the political order resonate with the radicality of someone whose vision was not precisely political. We need hermeneutics, which means understanding linked to historical context, and deconstruction, which means an interpretive theory that is mad about justice, in order to make this translation. Jesus lived in an occupied country in an obscure corner of the Roman empire. He was not a citizen in a modern representative political democracy, and he was not addressing people who bear the responsibility of citizens to vote. He knew nothing about democratic elections, the consequences of which reach profoundly into the lives of society's poorest and most defenseless people, who are the least represented group among those who actually do vote. We cannot know what Jesus would do in such an entirely different world as ours. In fact, as Garry

Wills says, we never know what Jesus was going to do next in the New Testament.[14] But we can use this question to put ourselves on the spot, to try to sensitize ourselves to the spirit of his life and teachings in the New Testament and then to employ as much good political, philosophical, and theological judgment as we can command in the present situation. That is why I have been calling on deconstruction to bring the good news of postmodern critique to the church. I think deconstruction is a congenial specter to the spirit of the kingdom and that it can sensitize the church to the Spirit that it breathes, or should breathe. (There is a historical reason for this congeniality, namely, the Jewish prophetic tradition, which links Jesus with the Jewishness of Levinas, who influenced Derrida, who was also Jewish.) Jesus thought that when all the large points and fine points of the Torah are taken into account, the law and the prophets come down to love of neighbor and of God, and he burned with anger when he thought the spirit of love was being undermined by inflexible rules or by hypocrisy. Love is the gift and love is not parsimonious. It does not dodge what is expected of it under the cover of rules or ideologies.

If St. Augustine really did say the following, I would quote it:

> What does love look like? It has the hands to help others. It has the feet to hasten to the poor and needy. It has eyes to see misery and want. It has the ears to hear the sighs and sorrows of men. That is what love looks like.

Unfortunately, the remark seems to come from a Hallmark card, but it is in any case a very nice line.[15] Now ask yourself, what does the Religious Right look like? Do they support a political vision that would expect the best of us, a vision that would inspire us to make economic sacrifices for the common good, for health care and the relief of poverty? Or do they support a political vision that underestimates the generosity of Americans and appeals to our greed by promising to reduce our taxes? Are they mad with their love of the poor and oppressed, or are they just plain mad because somebody is asking them to reach into their pockets?[16]

Instead of being eloquent advocates of a truly evangelical nation, one marked by generosity and self-sacrificing dedication to the least among us, a see-how-they-love-one-another Christianity, evangelical Christianity has instead been corrupted by unfettered capitalism, which rots our souls and our "family values"[17] more surely than drinking wine, which Jesus *did do*. (I am hoping that the historical-critical research people will show he also danced!) The Right thinks that the breakdown of the family is the source of crime and poverty, and this they very insightfully blame on the homosexuals, which would be amusing were it not so tragic. Families and "family values" are crushed by grinding poverty, which also makes violent crime and drugs attractive alternatives to desperate young men and sends young women into prostitution. Family values are no less corrupted by the corrosive effects of individualism, consumerism, and the accumulation of wealth. Instead of shouting this from the mountain tops, the get-me-to-heaven-and-the-rest-be-damned Christianity the Christian Right preaches is itself a version of selfish spiritual capitalism aimed at netting major and eternal dividends, and it fits hand in glove with American materialism and greed.

On this point, I am happy to say that a whole phalanx of progressive evangelical thinkers, led by Jim Wallis, Tony Campolo, Brian McLaren, (lately) Jimmy Carter, and many others, is exposing the ruse that passes itself off as the "Christian" Right even as they have rightly warned the Left about its congenital and dogmatic suspicion of religion.[18] The Left has still to learn from prophetic lives of men like Martin Luther King Jr. or Desmond Tutu or Óscar Romero that a movement for social justice, indeed a nation, has to have a soul and be led by people who believe in the impossible. But we have reason to hope that both the ruse of the Right and the dogmatism of the Left will not endure much longer. When this dual plague is over, we will ask ourselves how such self-deception about the gospel of Jesus was possible.

In the meantime, I am compelled to say, both these American offspring of the Reformers and my friends on the secular Left will have a good deal to learn from the Vatican. The papal social encyclicals are a model of Christian economics, of bringing the spirit of the gospels to bear on modern economic realities.[19] My Protestant friends on the Christian Right will finally find that they are surrounded on both sides—by Jacques Derrida and Jacques Maritain, by deconstruction and the pope, who are all mad about justice while they are simply mad about paying taxes. The encyclicals contain unambiguous warnings about the greed and insensitivity to the poorest and most defenseless people in our society that is bred by capitalism. They speak eloquently of the rights of workers, of the requirements for "social" checks on "individual" freedoms, and of the priority of the "common good" over egoism and individualism. I share the passion of the Reformers to rid themselves of papal imperialism. But I heartily recommend to my friends on the Christian Right—both Protestant and Catholic—a summer spent reading the Vatican's social encyclicals, in which they will find a good deal more of the spirit of the New Testament than presently parades around today on bumper stickers, bracelets, and T-shirts emblazoned with the name of Jesus. As a primer, start with Jacques Maritain's *Integral Humanism* if you want to learn a thing or two about how to get Christian faith and a concern for the common good inside the same head.[20]

Power and Violence

Now let us move up the I-95 corridor from Alabama to the Washington Beltway where, I dare say, a visit by Jesus would leave him no less nonplussed by what is going on in his name. Here I will take my point of departure from the claim made by George W. Bush that his favorite political philosopher is Jesus. In this resolve I must not allow myself to falter, since the messianic delusion in the Bush administration that Bush is God's appointed one suggests that the man is sincere,[21] and that has put the entire globe in danger. I pray that I will not be led into the temptation of believing that this claim is a cynical way of avoiding the admission that Bush has never read any political philosophy at all and will say just about anything as a way to justify that he actually thinks he is above the law. I pray for the strength to take him at his word. I pray, in the spirit of deconstruction, not to seek to ascertain the hidden intentions of the author, and, in the spirit of Christianity, to leave all judgment to God.

Historically, Christians were against war until God gave them the power to wage one (or so they think). Then God gave them the light to see the merits of a "just war," a phrase that should stick in the throat of any follower of Jesus. Just imagine the challenge Jesus would have faced trying to work "just war" into the Sermon on the Mount! If we recall the historical context of "just war" doctrine, then it is clear that the only just war is the war against war and the war we should have with ourselves on the matter of war. Indeed, the theory might be read as calling for no more war, on the grounds that hardly any war would ever be just. There is an admirable tradition of Christian pacifism exemplified by the Quakers, Mennonites, and Anabaptists—not to mention the *first* Christians themselves—for whom the contemporary moral theologians John Howard Yoder and Stanley Hauerwas are theological heroes for having eloquently made the case that the political import of the figure of Jesus in the New Testament is precisely pacifism. Exegetically, I think that conclusion is difficult to escape. If we were to actually craft a political view exclusively on the basis of the portrait we have of Jesus in the New Testament, we would be hard put to reach any *other* conclusion. Jesus said blessed are the peacemakers, not blessed are the makers of a just war. He said that if you are struck on one cheek, you should turn the other, not that you should make preemptive strikes to fend off such hits in advance. And when it was clear that his own life was lost, he asked the Father to forgive the Roman soldiers who were carrying out this cruel and unjust execution.[22]

So as near as I can tell, if you really intend to take the Jesus of the New Testament as a "political philosopher," then the tax rate would be 100 percent and the Department of Defense annual budget would be $0 (no swords). To which, we may add, surely Jesus would have second thoughts about capital punishment! Am I wrong, or is not the crucifixion Christianity's best argument against capital punishment (a category in which George Bush's Texas leads the nation, while the United States is right up there with Iran, North Korea, and China in the international lead)?

To be sure, radical pacifism does not prevent us from rising up in moral wrath and righteous protest against hypocrisy and injustice, like the prophets of old. Quite the opposite. When Jesus said, do you think I have come to bring peace, no I bring the sword (Matt. 10:34), when he said that he comes to bring fire and division (Luke 12:49–53), he did not mean a physical sword and arson. He saved physical violence for fig trees, a herd of pigs (which will anger the animal rights movement of today), and the money-changers' tables. He did mean that we must be prepared to endure the harshest difficulties in the pursuit of peace and justice, even to hating our father and our mother, which was his idea of "family values" in the kingdom.[23] He meant that we should be prepared to die for what is right, not that we should be prepared to kill. His word is hard, and who can bear it? His most characteristic sayings are a scandal to the world of Roman power, deeply paradoxical contradictions of the ways of *Realpolitik*—like offering a set of beatitudes that make a virtue out of meekness, mercy, humility, and poverty, everything the Roman world mocked and despised. The model that Jesus sets is impossible—precisely what Derrida would call *the* impossible—a theo-poetics of the impossible. It requires loving and forgiving what it is impossible to love or forgive, loving and forgiving your enemies, not just your friends. The most elemental fact of Christian political reflection is that nearly every existing form of Christianity, not to mention every existing nation-state, compromises "the impossible" that defines Christian love.

Just-war theory, first formulated by St. Augustine, is "Constantinianism," a post-Constantinian compromise of the gospel, formulated at a time when Christians sat on the throne of Rome instead of being dragged before it. The doctrine of just war, formulated four centuries after the death of Jesus, was the result of sitting down to table with the powers of this world. War looks different from the thrones of power than it does from the galleys of the persecuted. Just-war doctrine makes sense, but it weakens and attenuates what St. Paul called the folly (*moria*) of the cross. It adopts the views not of Jesus but of Cicero, not of the kingdom of God but of the Roman Empire. Just-war doctrine—the very expression, as Daniel Maguire says, is oxymoronic—is a worldly concession, not an evangelical counsel.[24] If the theory is meant to keep one eye on Jesus, a very squinting eye indeed since Jesus called for unconditional peace, it keeps another and much larger wide-open eye on the motto of a Roman general, *si vis pacem, para bellum* (if you want peace, get ready for war).

At the very least, the opposition to violence on the part of Jesus in the New Testament must be the context of any Christian reflection on war. True, St. Paul was prepared to see the sword wielded on those who broke the law (Rom. 13:4), but then again Paul practically never quoted a thing Jesus said. Our lives are largely a matter of negotiating the distance between the standard of absolute nonviolence that is set forth in the words and deeds of Jesus and the brutal reality of the world. Just-war doctrine is already a failure of faith, treating unconditional peace and forgiveness as simply impossible, even while repeating the words of Jesus that with God all things are possible.

I confess to being part of this, too. I do not think that absolute pacifism, which is central to the poetico-prophetic vision Jesus had of a life of unconditional love, can be translated one to one into a political order. But it is intended to provide the context and the spirit of a politics that is supposed to resonate with its uncondi-tionality. That is why I prefer to redescribe just-war theory as the "lesser-evil theory." The sorry truth is that sometimes resisting evil requires fighting back. I do not think of wars as "just" but rather as lesser evils, which, to that extent, are justified but without being just. We are justified in choosing the lesser evil, but that does not make the lesser evil just. At most, just-war theory offers justification without justice. As I have insisted throughout, we cannot simply look at what Jesus said and directly transcribe it into the present context. Jesus was speaking as a religious poet-prophet to people in an occupied land that was part of a vast empire over which they had no influence whatsoever. He was not trying to organize a political party or start a revolution. When the Jews did rise up against Rome, their temple was razed and they were scattered to the four winds. Today Christians in Western Europe and North America live in an entirely different situation—between England in the nineteenth century and the United States thereafter, the Anglophone world *is* the empire, in contradiction not only to the gospel but also to the very idea of a distribution of power and a system of checks and balances that define a democratic world order and community of nations. (We have seen the Roman Empire—and we are it!) The far Right's "evangelical" response to this is to champion the idea of a Christian Empire, of a Holy American Empire, a Pax Americana that is an unnerving correlate to the very Pax Romana that took the life of Jesus.[25]

I am saying all this about the nonviolence of Jesus to emphasize how infinitely delicate a Christian conscience must be about war. For any political view inspired by the vision of Jesus, war must be a nightmare, a last extreme measure resorted to because every other way has been cut off, because our backs are pinned to the wall, our very skin has become too tight and, God help us, there is no other way out. I do not want to reject just-war theory but I do want to hold it up against the white light of the New Testament and the call for unconditional peace announced there by Jesus.

But how should Christians, filled with Jesus's love of peace and nonviolence, judge the war in Iraq? Remember the stated principle:

Jesus is our guiding political philosopher! With this in mind, let us ask ourselves a series of important questions. Does this war embody the nonviolent ideals of the Christian gospel? Does it represent a sensitive application even of the later just-war doctrine? Or is it separated by an abyss from the Sermon on the Mount and by still a second abyss from the demands of the commonly received just-war doctrine of the church? Should not Christians regard war as a most harsh and extreme departure from evangelical ideals to be undertaken only because every other avenue had been explored, because no stone had been left unturned? Can a gospel of nonviolence embrace the very idea of a "preemptive" war? Has the demand of Christian ethics been met that war be a last resort, after every alternative is exhausted, when the very national security was at risk? Has the Christian demand for truth and honesty been met by those who have led us into this war and put so many lives at risk? Were the premises on which we entered this war confirmed or were they proven to be plainly false and, beyond false, do we not now suspect that they have been intentionally falsified? While no Christian can sanction the heinous dictatorship of Saddam Hussein, did Iraq pose a real and imminent threat to the people of the United States? Can a heart formed by the gospel of Christian love judge that the harm caused by this war is proportionate to the evil we proposed to relieve? Can Christians, who affirm the sanctity of life and who repeat the words of Jesus that he was sent by God "to proclaim release to the captives" (Luke 4:18), be silent in the face of the torture, abuse, and unlawful detention of prisoners? Where is the figure of Jesus in a war that has cost the lives of thousands of American and Iraqi soldiers, of countless innocent noncombatants, women and children, and has razed countless homes, hospitals, and schools, and caused untold suffering to an innocent civilian population, driving a large portion of Iraqi families into exile or domestic displacement and reducing their country to civil war? Is the cause of the peace of Christ served by a war that all the evidence indicates has provided a rallying call for anti-American radicals throughout the Middle East and has made the lives of everyone in the Middle East, Western Europe, and the United States not more secure but less? Was justice rendered against the true perpetrators of 9/11 or has the war proven to be a diversion from pursuing them, a diversion that has allowed them to regroup in Afghanistan? Where is the figure of Jesus in this national policy? How is Jesus the "political philosopher" who inspired the architects of this war? Where is the Christian witness for peace and nonviolence in this national debate? I find it impossible to avoid the conclusion that countless other Christians have reached: in this war there is neither what the papal encyclicals call *jus ad bellum* nor what they call *jus in bello*—there was neither a just cause in going to war nor a just execution of the war.

Strategically, diplomatically, socially, politically, morally, economically, evangelically, in every possible way, we are witness today to a low point in American leadership, an ethical, social, political, and biblical catastrophe. Jesus would hardly recognize himself, and I also doubt that Cicero would! Instead of denouncing such policies in no uncertain terms, in the classic prophetic tradition of the Bible, the Christian Right cheers them on. Instead of serving as the prophetic voice of Amos giving President Jeroboam holy hell, instead of being the voice of Jesus and of the gospel in an act of unilateral American military aggression, the Christian Right dreams of a Christian Empire.

Once again, I find it necessary to direct these sons and daughters of the Reformation to the statements of the American Catholic Conference of Bishops and to the various Vatican pronouncements that have declared this war unjust in no uncertain terms.[26] Not only is the Christian Right's bumper-sticker Jesus a cheerleader for lowering the taxes of the wealthy, but their Jesus is also a militarist. If we ask, "What would Jesus deconstruct?" about many Christian churches, my own guess is that he would not know where to start—with their militarism and imperialism or with their greed and indifference to the poor. The closest thing they represent to anything Jesus encountered in his own lifetime was called "Rome." He simply would not recognize himself. But you can count on it, if he reappeared in their midst protesting the war in Iraq, he would be spotted and denounced as a left-wing radical, a deconstructor, who has come back, uninvited, to make trouble for the church, and then subjected to a vicious smear campaign by wealthy right-wing "Christians."

In Her Steps

The next theological feather that requires ruffling is patriarchy, which in deconstruction means the theory that man is to be defined as plenitudinous presence and woman as missing something (guess what!), a theory that richly deserves reversal and displacement. To that end, let's start with the case of Dan Brown's *The Da Vinci Code*, a fun read and a thriller that has wrankled the Catholic Church in particular. The church's strong reaction to a work of manifest fiction suggests that the book steps on a theological third rail, the sexuality of Jesus! That Jesus would have married and had a child! The church is all for the "Incarnation" and for *deus verus et homo verus*, but not that much flesh, not anything that incarnate, not that human. (I do not even mention Mary Immaculate, who does not get to conceive Jesus by human means, share in original sin, or die a mortal death before being assumed into heaven!) Moreover, however fanciful its speculations, *The Da Vinci Code* reminds us that it is no fancy that much of what Jesus said and did is lost in the fog of history. There are many interpretations of what he actually said and did, and both the New Testament itself and the "orthodox" Nicene theology of the later church are just two of them, a point that unsettles the long-robed powers that be (*ta onta!*) all the way down to their episcopal toes. In deconstruction, the New Testament is an archive, not the arche,[27] and to mix up the two, as the fundamentalists do, is to make an idol out of an icon. Deconstruction saves us from idolatry, while scriptural literalism succumbs to the idolatry of a book.

I am hardly arguing for the historicity of Brown's novel, but I do agree with a friend of mine who said, "What's the big deal? It's not a deal breaker!" Even scholars who reject outright or who simply suspend the question of the divinity of Jesus think that he had the lifestyle of a celibate prophet, not of a married man with a family. That's not the issue. The issue—in addition to the threat it poses to mandatory celibacy—is whether the church can deal with the fact that a woman would have been that important in the life of Jesus, that a woman would have been an intimate or at least an important disciple of Jesus or would have played an important role in his life and in the life of the early church. Indeed given Jesus's habits of improbable association—with tax collectors, sinners, prostitutes—that is not so improbable. When it comes to research on Jesus, improbability is a mark of probability, of authenticity; when he said or did something unusual, that is most likely to stand out and be remembered and to be based on an authentic tradition. The story of the woman at the well is interesting on many levels, one of which is that he was talking to her at all, which fell well outside the usual protocols of the time. But that seems to be the sort of thing he did all the time.

Of course, patriarchy is not the exclusive province of the church; it seems to be older than God. It is found everywhere, East or West, Athens or Jerusalem, antiquity or modernity. With a few notable exceptions here and there, it has been the way of the world, the oldest "common sense," or "natural law" the world has known, from which we have been only gradually and imperfectly able to twist free. The role of the church in all this is typically ambiguous. On the one hand, the church has been a veritable fortress of patriarchy, giving divine sanction to sexism by serving up a heavenly patriarchy as a model for the rule of earthly fathers. The Bible has been invoked more times than we care to think to oppress women, which has led secular feminists to take it out to the shed. On the other hand, precisely as deconstruction predicts, there is something else going on in the church, and especially in a text as rich as the New Testament. The church is a bastion of patriarchy but it also harbors the kingdom of God, which undermines patriarchy.

The treatment of women in the church has been well and rightly worked over by secular feminism. But the patriarchal church also falls afoul of the very spirit of the gospel, which is to treat with a special evangelical privilege the people on the short end of the stick of historical power, the nothings and the nobodies, *ta me onta*, which is the madness of the Good News that defies the world. Patriarchy is contradicted by what Alain Badiou and others today call the "universalism" of St. Paul, who said in Galatians that there is neither male nor female, Jew nor Greek, free man nor slave.[28] This universalism means first a reversal of this invidious hierarchy, then displacement—neither male nor female. What better example is there of the paradoxical logic of God's ways, which are marked by a kind of deconstructive subversion of the human order of being, presence, power, and wisdom, than a reversal of patriarchal values, which reflect nothing so much as the business-as-usual of the world? If God makes the wisdom of the world foolish, then God makes the worldly wisdom of subordinating women to men foolish, and if the one who boasts should boast only in the Lord, then he has no business boasting in masculinity, which more often than not is nothing to boast about. Does not God choose the women to confound the pride and power of men? Is that not how things are done in the kingdom of God? Is that not the "event" that stirs within the name of God, which reverses human priorities in favor of God's? What Paul is saying in 1 Corinthians 11, when he backs off the radicality of the trail he is blazing in 1 Corinthians 1, has no more to do with the kingdom of God than does the pre-Copernican cosmology of the First Letter to the Thessalonians, in which Paul tells us that Jesus is going to come down on a cloud and gather up those who are still living and open the graves and then carry everyone up into the sky. That might have been a way to make a point in the middle of the first century CE, but it has since lost its punch. It has no more plausibility than saying that man was not made from woman but woman from man (1 Cor. 11:8), which has also turned out to be a masculine fantasy, men having been woven from a watery womanly womb right from the start.

Jesus appears to have acted as if the kingdom of God bestows a certain freedom on us that the church, instituted in his name, proved quick to shut down. So if the church would make itself transparent to the kingdom that it is called to proclaim, it would renounce its patriarchy and proclaim that, as a part of the panoply of reversals brought about in the poetics of the kingdom, God chose women to shame the vainglory of men. Secularist feminists, by contrast, would do well to follow the example of Luce Irigaray, who recognized the overlapping concerns of her work with feminist theologians like Elizabeth Schüssler Fiorenza.[29] The church should joyfully embrace the discipleship of equals, the discipleship of women, who are no less called (*kletos*) to proclaim the kingdom than men, no less admissible to teach and instruct and baptize and lead in worship than the boys! I like to point out that for Derrida the best way to undertake a deconstruction, to expose the cracks and fissures in a thing while also opening it to its own future, is to write a detailed microhistory of the subject. But any careful historical analysis will show, as numerous feminist studies confirm,[30] that women clearly were to be found among leaders of the early church and were not always relegated to secondary positions. The subsequent failure of the church to ordain women is an insult to and a contradiction of the ministry of Jesus, violating not only its spirit but also its early history. As Schüssler Fiorenza might put it, the memory of him should not exclude the memory of her.

The sanctifying power that issues from the life and death of Jesus is not gendered. Let us ask ourselves, in all honesty, what makes Jesus the icon of the living God. The fact that he spoke Aramaic, was of such and such a height or weight, had eyes and hair and skin of a certain color, was left handed or right handed? That he was masculine not feminine? Would it not be a case of the most unvarnished idolatry to fix on one of them as a mark of God? What more odious and obvious, more conspicuous and embarrassing spectacle of idolatry in the church than to conflate the masculinity of Jesus with the image of God, with the iconic way he bears the coming of the kingdom in his words and deeds? Can a more ancient, more deeply entrenched and more transparent idol be imagined? Freudians make a career out of what the human psyche makes of the phallus (or the other way around!). It would almost be amusing were it not so serious! If the church insists on the masculinity of Jesus, or of God, does that get us back to the mystery of the "wholly other"? Is that the step/not beyond or just plain theological flat-footedness? Do we feel ourselves thereby envisaged by God or are we just looking in the mirror? Do we honor the life-transforming power of Jesus or a patriarchal model borrowed from the Greco-Roman household? Is the loyalty of the biblical religions to a male clergy loyalty to Jesus or simply the loyalty of the boys to themselves?

Now ask yourself: What would Jesus deconstruct?[31]

Large White Elephants

The underlying problem in all of this, as I see it, is the large white elephant in the room that I have not mentioned yet, abortion and homosexuality, which actually make two large white elephants. Good and decent people have lost their ethical equilibrium and contracted all their moral energy into a single issue or two that drive all the other issues, including more important ones. The ethical and political voice of the church has been distorted and drained by issues surrounding sexuality and marriage while violence and poverty are left to fester like unattended diseases in the body of the church. It is argued, for example, that there are about 1.3 million induced abortions each year in the United States,[32] which is therefore a proportionately graver issue than the war in Iraq where, even granting the highest estimates made by opponents of the war, some 250,000 people have been killed.[33] But if you want to play such a gruesome numbers game, reflect for a moment on the unthinkable catastrophe that awaits us if nuclear weapons get into this act. Furthermore, UNICEF reports that worldwide over 10 million children die of hunger and poverty every year, which represents a horror of still greater proportions, about which the Right invests no comparable moral outrage, time, or money, not to mention the nearly half-million children who died from HIV/AIDS in 2006, or the 12 million orphaned by the disease, simply because they are too poor to afford the medications they require.[34] It is one thing to insist on the right to be born but quite another to effectively abandon these and many more children to the harshest of fates after birth, all while having the name of "Jesus" and the "sanctity of life" on one's lips.

This makes for a perfect political storm. As Jim Wallis and others point out, the Left is blind to the prophetic resources of the Scriptures while the Christian Right suffers from a kind of moral tunnel vision as abortion and homosexual rights issues monopolize and monocularize the wider moral vision of the church. No one issue has been more instrumental in making "Reagan Democrats" and right-wing Republicans out of large numbers of American Catholics, otherwise the bearers of enlightened social teachings by the popes and bishops, and the contemporary descendants of historically poor European immigrants, who had earlier migrated straight into the Democratic Party and the New Deal. Along with the opposition to gay and lesbian rights—Karl Rove's favorite hammer for galvanizing the far-right base—the opposition to abortion rights has lined up the churches squarely against everything that Jesus said about peace and poverty. It is into that very large storm that I now steer this little craft.

Homosexuality

About homosexuality Jesus said and did nothing that we know of, but we can guess what he thought. The Jews of Jesus's time differed from the Greeks on several issues, one of which was that the Greeks permitted love between men, practiced under certain definite constraints, while the Jews did not. I appreciate the scholarly work that has been recently undertaken to interpret what the Scriptures have said about homosexuality and I wish it well.[35] But even were this research not to hold up, I could live with the idea that Paul condemned what we today have constituted as "homosexuality" and that if anyone ever asked Jesus about it (and if they did we have no record of it) he would have said the same thing as Paul. Indeed, had Jesus anything new to say on the subject I imagine that this would have been so astonishing that it would have been remembered and made its way into the record.

In my view, even if there is a dominant view against homosexuality in the Scriptures and tradition—and as a deconstructive reader, I would always insist on a full hearing for all the nondominant views, of which there are plenty—I would argue that on this point the Greeks were right and the dominant tradition among Jews and Christians is wrong, just as the Scriptures are wrong to underwrite slavery and the oppression of women. Indeed, by invoking the spirit of a certain Jesus, I would argue for a counterfactual conditional: were Jesus alive today and familiar with the pros and cons of the contemporary argument, his centeredness on love would have brought him down on the side of the rights of what we today call the "homosexual" difference (which is not necessarily the same phenomenon that is being described in the Scriptures, as Dale Martin argues[36]). After my friends on the Right have regained consciousness, they will perhaps want to hear my reasons for saying this. Jesus systematically took the side of the outsider, of those who are excluded and marginalized and made to suffer for their marginalization by the powers that be, those whose names are blackened by their difference from the mainstream. Based on the gospel of love by which he was driven, he would today have found love in homosexual love and a mission among the advocates of gay and lesbian rights. But counterfactual conditionals do not settle much. We need to think through this issue for ourselves on the conjoined basis of critical reasoning and the spirit of Jesus.[37]

Of homosexuality itself, apart from prooftexting the New Testament, I think the independent ethical arguments against it fail. Those arguments tend to boil down to an essentialist idea of "human nature" that usually turns out to be the historically contingent idea of human beings held by those with the power to define what being human means. Here Derrida's earlier work in *Of Grammatology*, which dealt with the constructedness and hence the deconstructibility of the distinction between culture and nature, and Foucault's notion of "power/knowledge" are particularly pertinent. The most famous, or infamous, example of the fragility of the case for natural law is the defense of the "natural slave" that goes back to Aristotle and Plato, who liked to think of human beings as graded metals: gold, silver, and brass. The slaves are low-grade natures, fitted out by nature to serve. Aristotle thinks slaves are "rational animals," of course, but that means that they are able to understand and follow a command but not to give one, a point that was also made about the "nature" of women. So the rule of men over slaves and women is an order dictated by nature itself, where it is the men who have the power to define what "nature" means, which is very convenient for the men. Natural law *theory* is notorious for serving the interests of the natural law *theorists*, for starting with a conclusion and then working back to the idea of "nature" that provides them with a suitable cover. That is "power/knowledge," not knowledge as power, but having the power to constitute what counts as knowledge.

A good deal of nature is fierce, heartless, and lethal. Tsunamis are natural. Animals feeding off the lives of other animals is natural. Nature aborts fetuses and kills off the weakest members of species. We must suspect ourselves and suspect that a good deal of what we mean by "nature" is sentimentality—or a cover for our will, a ruse under which we cloak how we ourselves want things to fall out. So we have to worry whenever "nature" is invoked and treat it with a certain measure of hermeneutic suspicion. The word "natural," like the question "What would Jesus do?" often functions as a club to pound what is different, to smash anything that falls outside the tolerances of the powers that be or the historical prejudices of the day. My own view is that the outcome of a careful debate about these matters would be to show that there simply are no arguments to show that homosexual love is of itself anything else than love, and that therefore, since the essence of the Torah is love, it hardly falls afoul of the law. To be sure, when it is not love, when it is promiscuity, or infidelity to a sworn partner, or rape, or the sexual abuse of minors, or in any way violent, then it is indeed not love, but that is no less true of heterosexuality.

An interpretation like this raises the question of the status of the Scriptures for me. My answer is that I am not an idolater. In deconstruction, the Scriptures are an archive, not the arche (which means they are not God). I take the second commandment very seriously and I do not put false gods—like books (biblical inerrantism) or the Vatican (papal infallibility)—before God, who is the "wholly other." I treat scriptural literalism like papal infallibility, as idolatry. To protect myself against the idolatry of the b(B)ook, I embrace the distinction made by Elizabeth Schüssler Fiorenza, which is very congenial to Derrida's distinction between arche and archive, between the Bible as a "timeless archetype" and the Bible as an historical "prototype." The former views the Bible as something that can be directly and decontextually copied and pasted into the present, while the latter understands the Bible to be something that must be hermeneutically interpreted, inserted with hermeneutic sensitivity into a contemporary context, similar to what Aristotle called the "schema" that stands in need of application in the concrete. This requires what Schüssler Fiorenza calls a "canon within the canon" to sort out the genuinely revelatory from time-bound prejudices and social constructions. That is pretty much what I mean by saying that the New Testament is a theo-poetics, not a politics, and that it is up to us to translate it into a praxis. This is why I started out by distinguishing words from the *events* that they harbor.[38] What is revealed in the Scriptures is not a literal picture to hold up against the present like a mechanical template but a living Spirit whose inner force is to be brought to bear in a loving and living dialogue with the circumstances of the present. Texts, Hans-Georg Gadamer liked to say, are like musical scores: you don't get music until somebody plays them, that is, reads and interprets the score.[39] On those grounds, Schüssler Fiorenza rightly says, no text "that perpetuates violence against women, children, or slaves should be accorded the status of divine revelation if we do not want to turn the God of the Bible into a God of violence."[40] That is, if you don't want to turn God into an idol of human fabrication. What is and what is not revelation is not a settled matter, and nothing is settled by a literal citation of the Bible or by quoting a Vatican document without a good stiff critical argument to go along with it.

I advocate a certain deconstructive reading of the scriptural text, which always means to be attuned to love while staying tuned to present circumstances. As St. Augustine actually does say:

> So if it seems to you that you have understood the divine Scriptures, or any part of them, in such a way that by this understanding you do not build up this twin love of God and neighbor, then you have not yet understood them.[41]

We need be no more guided by the letter of what the Scriptures say about homosexuality than we are by what they say about slavery or geocentrism, which reflect the circumstances of their composition, not the spirit of the kingdom that comes to contradict the world.

Release from idolatry is the part of the relief, the good news, that postmodernity offers to the church. The Scriptures, in turn, do not relieve us of the responsibility of thinking for ourselves (*sapere aude*) or of rethinking ancient traditions, for the ultimate tradition that is handed down to us is not any particular creed, practice, or institutional structure, but the *event* of love that was astir in Jesus and then is handed on to the church. Derrida would say that a genuine tradition is not constituted by any position or positivity but by a deeper affirmation. The task is not to reproduce literally what Jesus said and did—I have never even seen an olive garden or a fig tree—but to repeat the love with which he said and did them, on the bet that those are the practices in which he would recognize himself today.[42]

Abortion

I have saved the most delicate issue for last because I myself have no brief to make on behalf of abortion. I approach the willful killing of anything—animals or enemies, felons or fetuses—with considerable fear and trembling. I treat abortion analogously to the way I treat just-war theory, as a lesser evil. When it is legally permissible, it is permissible as the lesser evil, which is, alas, the way too much of our ethical existence falls out. When it is permissible, that has to do with a legal right to choose. The legal right to choose to have an abortion is not an ethical judgment of approval of abortion but an ethical judgment of approval of the freedom and dignity of choice. The choice is justified but that does not make abortion just. Life is not just. To be sure, on a Derridean analysis, laws are supposed to be just and justice is supposed to have the force of law, but Derrida's point is that this gap can never close. Still, I have no business advocating laws that permit what I consider to be unjust. I have no confidence in a simple opposition of what is legal and what is ethical. Nor do I see the legal to be a neutral or value-free zone as opposed to the value-laden sphere of ethics. Nothing is neutral. The legal seems to me to be the ethical about which we can strike an agreement, where there is a consensus about justice. There is a consensus about murder, theft, and rape that makes them uncontroversial matters of regulation by law. When abortion is permitted under *certain* circumstances but not all, as most obviously when the life of the mother is threatened, it is because the ethical consensus about freedom of choice in that circumstance is stronger than the ethical consensus about banning abortions under *all* circumstances. I also readily concede that someone can make a perfectly sensible use of Derrida's analysis of the "force of law" to oppose the right to choose on the grounds that such a "law" violates the "justice" due the unborn, who is the defenseless other. My view is that the optimal demands of justice are met by laws that restrict access to abortions under some circumstances and protect freedom of choice in other circumstances. Hermeneutics is inescapable. Hermeneutics, radical hermeneutics, goes all the way down.

Abortion is always a bad and difficult choice, but making a bad choice is better than making a worse one, and sometimes making a bad choice is better than being forbidden to choose at all. Abortion is violence; it takes life. Let that be said, and unambiguously. Abortion should send a shudder down the spine of anyone who affirms the model of nonviolence set forth by Jesus in the New Testament and anyone who takes seriously the notion of children as exemplars of the kingdom. Just so, it should unnerve anyone who in the spirit of deconstruction's love of justice is worried about violence against the defenseless other. It should unnerve any lover of deconstruction, which I have described as an account of events, where things are pregnant with and expectant of the event, and where the idea of aborting the event is an abomination. But nothing is simple, nothing is just black and white, no one can ever consistently say, "Thou shalt not kill," which is also a crucial idea in deconstruction, which I am reading as the hermeneutics of the kingdom of God. To say the least, the issue is complex.

Let us start by looking to what Jesus said and did. No special concern about abortion is expressed in the Jewish Scriptures and we have no record that Jesus ever expressed himself about it or took exception with the prevailing view of the day; if he had we would likely have heard of it.[43] We do know that Jesus was sharply critical of hypocrisy, and that is the point I would like to visit in particular. In my view, it is hypocritical for Christians to oppose abortion while endorsing capital punishment[44] and preemptive wars. It is hypocritical to populate the killing fields of poverty by aligning oneself with, or even remaining silent about, policies that exacerbate economic and social injustice, which seed and cultivate the fields of abortion. Prosperous and educated people normally have the know-how and the resources to avoid unwanted pregnancies. The most consistent and sensible position in this regard is the "seamless garment" argument against violence of any stripe made by Cardinal Bernardin: the right to life spans the entire spectrum and it includes not only fetuses but felons, not only friends but enemies, "from womb to tomb."[45] Christian witness requires a radical opposition to violence in all its forms and seeing the interconnectedness of such opposition.

It is hypocritical to oppose abortion while simultaneously opposing the vast support system such a ban would require. That would include full and free prenatal care of poor and uninsured pregnant women, of unemployed and unwed mothers, so that they might bring their pregnancies safely to full term, along with free neonatal care for their uninsured children. It would further include a comprehensive system of government-supported adoption agencies in order to place newborn children in welcoming families when the birth mothers are unable or unwilling to care for their children. It would include a comprehensive system of day care that would support working unwed mothers who wish to keep their children and a dramatic increase in support for the public schools in the poorest neighborhoods that these children will attend, instead of letting these children fall off the radar as soon as they *are* born. All that would require funding, which means taxes, which conflicts with the greed of the Right, religious and secular. Beyond that, the working families into which children are born need to be protected by fair labor laws, living wages, medical and vacation benefits, and good pension funds. The latter in turn need to be protected from corporate criminals who run companies into the ground while giving themselves extravagant salaries and severance packages and letting the hardworking employees who lose their jobs and their pensions end up paying the price for the criminals' misdeeds.

Furthermore, the number of unwanted pregnancies, and therefore of abortions, could be reduced, probably quite sharply, by easy access to safe and sensible means of artificial contraception, to which the Catholic Church is opposed.[46] Philosophically, this opposition has nothing whatsoever to do with Jesus. It arises from Stoic "natural law" theory, where artificial birth control is taken to violate the "intention of nature."[47] The theory was proposed at a time when the only real way to meet the threat to the species posed by a plague or natural disaster was to produce enough offspring to survive the ensuing decimation. Today the situation is exactly the opposite: the threat posed to the species by overpopulation and overtaxing the earth's resources is real and potent while underpopulation is no threat at all. This is a lucid example of Derrida's point that if a law is not deconstructible it becomes a monster. On the one hand, I agree that nothing is to be gained from having adolescents become sexually active before they are ready, but that has a lot to do with the culture of greed and wealth that the Right promotes. To argue, on the other hand, that the use of artificial contraception methods, even among married couples, violates the intention of nature can result only in giving the impression that to be a Christian is to check your rational faculties at the door. One might as well argue that umbrellas are unnatural because they frustrate the intention of nature to make us wet, or that central heating systems are unnatural because they frustrate the intention of the winter to freeze us to death. When these arguments are extended to denying the distribution of condoms in sub-Saharan Africa, where in some countries fully a third of the population suffers from HIV/AIDS, an unreasonable position becomes Kafkaesque.[48]

Finally, I think there is an irreducible but loose law of inverse proportions between the legal rights of a pregnant woman to make choices about what is going on in her own body and the rights of the fetus to life: with each passing day the latter grows stronger, and at some point, which cannot be exactly defined or programmed, a line is crossed in which the weight of justice and the ethics of the other—of defending the weak against the strong—shifts to the side of the defenseless and unborn fetus. Before that point, in a civil, democratic, and pluralistic society, women should have the legal right to choose what to do, and abortion should be safe, legal, and rare, as Bill Clinton said—and Bill looks better with every passing day. In a perfect world, there is no such tension; but the world is not perfect. The early church, from the Didache on, condemned abortion, but later on, as the influence of Aristotle made itself felt, some distinctions began to be introduced that reflected a sense of this moving point.[49]

Abortion at any stage offends a sensitive conscience; it is always a difficult, bad, and traumatic choice. But all too often ethical life comes down to choosing the lesser of two evils, and we are not afforded the luxury of choosing an undiluted good. I argued this point some years ago under the controversial title *Against Ethics*, which invoked the example of a certain Yeshua.[50] Life is not organized into binary blacks and whites but inevitably serves up an ambiguous and graded scale of grays. What the least bad thing to do is in the earlier stages of an unwanted pregnancy, in the very singular circumstances in which each woman or teenage girl finds herself, too often in an impossible situation and faced with an impossible choice, is a matter of personal conscience. The demands of love and justice are self-conflicted in those situations. There is no one right answer. Life is not fair. I understand why many Christians would want to discourage women from ever choosing to have an abortion in any circumstance. But such people have the responsibility to put their money where their faith is, to do everything they can to provide these women and the children they will bear with a comprehensive system of support, and to address the deeper structural issues of poverty that spawn so many unwanted pregnancies. But then, when all that is said and done, above all in a democratic and pluralistic society, they need to respect the freedom of the other, which is irreducible, and to avoid religious imperialism.

That is precisely why I do not think that, given the spirit of love and forgiveness Jesus embodied, we would find him among the anti-abortion marchers of today. My best guess is that Jesus would be offended by the hypocrisy of a good many of these protesters and merciful about the difficult choice with which women are faced. What would Jesus do were he to come on an abortion clinic surrounded by an angry crowd of protesters? We do not know. But we do know how he dealt with another angry crowd gathered around a woman. What if these angry protesters also protest efforts to restrain the right to bear arms and eliminate capital punishment? If they rally noisily around an unjustified preemptive war that has made the world even more dangerous than it was on the morning of 9/11? What if they cheer on those who endanger the lives and health of present and future generations by a reckless abuse of the environment?[51] What if after all this shouting they suddenly lose their voice when it comes to addressing the brutal poverty in which unwanted pregnancies abound and by which families are crushed? What if they champion public policies that effectively abandon these children as soon as they are born to the cruelest social and economic conditions? What if they do not say a word about a world where many millions more children die of starvation and AIDS? Faced with accusers like that, with their stones piled high, my best bet is that Jesus would stoop down, write on the sidewalk, and scatter them.

6

The Working Church

Notes on the Future

If this book is trying to bring the good news of postmodernism to the church, and if the church is a real institution, and if we will always have institutions—like the poor—with us, then it behooves me to address the church's real institutional life and to talk a little bit about its future. That I intend to do by presenting two case studies, two concrete instances of church life, which I propose for special commendation and imitation. In cases like these, I hope to show, a certain church is alive and well—and, I would wager, always has been—in marginal Christian communities, out of power and out of the limelight, where the task of inscribing the mark of Jesus on the world is carried out quietly and without a lot of fanfare. Here are concrete cases where the deconstructive energies that I want to call on to till the soil of the life of the church in the twenty-first century hit the ground. I am a philosopher, not a pastor—you may have noticed!—and I have no interest in or competency for writing a manual for pastors. But, in my view from the pews, I want to draw attention to the life and practices of two communities on which I place an exemplary value, two places where I think something important, something paradigmatic, is going on. Here, for my money (so to speak), the kingdom of God is being proclaimed in uniquely deconstructive tones or, alternately, deconstruction is being deployed under the name of the kingdom. Here, in either case, the question "What would Jesus deconstruct?" is translated into the concrete.

Theo-Praxis: Diary of a City Priest

I began this little book with Charles Sheldon's *In His Steps*, a reflection on the state of Christianity at the dawn of the twentieth century (1896) by a working pastor, so it is fitting to draw this book to a conclusion by taking up something of a contemporary counterpart to Sheldon's book. *Diary of a City Priest* was written almost exactly a hundred years later, at the dawn of the twenty-first century (1993), by John McNamee, another working pastor, this one a Catholic priest who runs St. Malachy's Church in North Philadelphia.[1] His book chronicles a year in his life as pastor of a church located in one of the most dangerous ghettos in North America, and it carries out a "deconstruction of the church" simply by telling the unvarnished truth of daily life in his parish. This parish could easily have supplied the setting for the award winning series *The Wire*, which is set in inner-city Baltimore—even the architecture of tiny brick rowhouses is the same—to which I referred in chapter 1. It describes the living counterpart, as in living hell, to Sheldon's "Tennesseetown," compounded tenfold by the proliferation of guns and drugs, which are more toxic than alcohol. The cover design of *Diary of a City Priest* contains a (fittingly) black and white photo of the stark ghetto neighborhood (not a smarmy Jesus). The ghettos of Los Angeles, McNamee thinks, with their separate bungalows and little lawns seem "tame" compared to "the impacted rowhouse landscape of Philadelphia" (*Diary*, 149), the inferno of brick houses that explode with heat in the dangerous inner-city summers whose onset everyone dreads. You get a good sense for this scenery from the 2001 film by the same name starring David Morse (now available in a 2003 DVD). The film's budget is modest but Morse's brooding, melancholy, self-doubting manner is exactly right for the role of "Mac"—as opposed to the Henry Fonda or Jimmy Stewart type we imagined for *In His Steps*.

This is a diary of marginality. St. Malachy's exists on "the margins of the Church" (*Diary*, 108). "The Church"—the Big one—is about bishops, clerical changes, the gossip in the diocesan news-paper, and fund-raising campaigns, and McNamee stays as far away as possible from its "tribal life." The "neighborhood" is about people who need detoxification programs, jobs, a priest to testify at a bail hearing or in night court, or a handout for food or an unpaid bill, which may actually be spent on drugs. It is about help-ing people without health insurance get admitted to a hospital, or about a ride home in the middle of the night, the priest being the one with a car (eventually stolen). It is about visiting people living in squalor with crying children, ten bodies squeezed inside two or three rooms with little or no furniture, about answering a rectory phone and doorbell that ring day and night, and the such. The archdiocese leaves him at his post because these neighborhoods, the people who live and die here, what they say or what he says to them, are not important. Why not? "No money. No Catholics. A world of Samaritans and publicans who do not count" (*Diary*, 118).

But there are two churches, the Big, visible one on top, with bishops, buildings, power, and photocopying machines, "all the hierarchical and theological nonsense" (*Diary*, 59), and another one underneath, down in the underbelly of the kingdom of God, in the streets, among *ta me onta*:

> The part of the Church that connects with everything here is the Gospel, and whatever else the Church gives or does not give, she does give me the Gospel, that strange story about publicans and prostitutes coming to the wedding feast while the obvious candi-dates are cast out. The Good Samaritan is the fellow who helps the bleeding man, and he is neither priest nor Levite. The Roman centurion has more faith about the cure of his servant than any faith appearing in the Chosen People. (*Diary*, 117–18)

This second church, what he calls "the working church," is left on its own to face a brutal world. "The trouble is that [here] the Scriptures have the same fragile, unreal quality as the Blessed Sacrament" (*Diary*, 110). McNamee survives in part by occasion-ally escaping to the green mountains of ancestral Donegal or by stealing time for the poetry of Gerard Manley Hopkins, two tem-porary respites from the trash-ridden rubble of North Philadel-phia. Once, while on retreat in Ireland, he meets "a gentle Irish Sister," with whom he shares a meal. This sister, whose religious order serves delinquent girls and prostitutes, some of whom actually became members of the order ("Magdalenes"), now works among the poorest women in Belfast. "Perhaps the real Church worth saving or belonging to is the Church represented by my table companion." The bureaucratic Church, the hierarchy, live off the "selfless miracle" of this woman "like parasites. . . . The people support them and their nonsense because when those who still do believe and contribute see the working Church, they see this quiet Sister, and they as well as I can believe in her" (*Diary*, 60). Two churches: the owners of the church, who have all the power, and the working church, whose only power is the power of powerlessness that commands our faith. "So I . . . know why Jesus became enraged at religious leaders. . . . He was shouting at them that publicans and prostitutes would enter the kingdom before the clergy" (*Diary*, 123).

This is a diary of *the* impossible. "I rage against the impossibility of my life. The rage is always there just below the surface, even when things seem smooth and I feel in control" (*Diary*, 115). Against "the impossibility of these neighborhoods where so much is in chaos. So many fractured lives, so many crises. . . . Nobody does anything until things fall apart and then they want or need me right away" (*Diary*, 116). Nothing works, everything is mayhem (*Diary*, 135). He is not angry with his people, but with himself for his impatience with them, with the impossibility of his life, of what he is asked to do, which can't be done, and more so with what these desperately poor people are asked to do, which can't be done. The neighborhoods are ruined by drugs, but the most he and the sisters he works with can do is chase the drug dealers. Nobody is interested in having them arrested and put in the system; the prisons are brutal, brutalizing, and only make matters worse (*Diary*, 188). Across the Delaware River, in Camden, New Jersey, where "the wreckage of urban sprawl without relief" is just as bad, another Irish priest runs a parallel parish. When the retired bishop of Camden dies, his ring and pectoral cross are stolen from the corpse during the night by a homeless man and a thirteen-year-old boy. The symbolism is powerful. In this world of "people wandering the streets stealing or taking anything moveable, hustling, scheming, conspiring, hanging out, drugging," we should not be surprised at how meaningless are the ornaments of a church and its bishops who "ignore the conditions which make life impossible" (*Diary*, 120–21). This is not to say that sometimes the impossible does not happen—"I pray at Mass for the impossible" (*Diary*, 156). Sometimes people hang on, sometimes a man who made a serious mistake and has turned himself around is granted parole or a hospital bed or a methadone clinic is found for someone at the edge of despair.

This is a diary that has ditched Cartesian certitudes, in which the Feast of Thomas the Doubter is a special one, "the disciple who had such difficulty believing the whole impossible story of the Resurrection. I know that difficulty" (*Diary*, 135). In a situation like this, faith is impossible, *the* impossible; one is called on to have faith in a world in which it is impossible to believe anything. Even when he prays he "just presumes the possibility or likelihood that no one is there. Never was, in any satisfying sense" (*Diary*, 135). With Graham Greene—he himself is something of a Graham Greene character—he thinks doubt is more human than faith, and a more self-doubting church would be more humane, the lack of doubt being the fuel for fanaticism. He must be careful not to let his doubts assault the faith of the people whom he has been sent to nourish, but he doubts a "specious theology" and a church that makes a "specious distinction between our several responsibilities to people up here [North Philadelphia] according to whether they are Catholics or not" (*Diary*, 137). He admires, with no little irony, the ability of the church to suppress doubt, to ignore the horrors of these ghettos, and to let all its "moral passion and vigor and insight" get absorbed by "our horror of abortion" (*Diary*, 187). When he prays, "two forces within me ebb and flow. . . . Nothing is out there. No one. Never was. The affect I bring to prayer because of my story [his personal biography and affectivity]. . . . The other is that sense which seems deeper and stronger: love has you here at all, sustains you, draws you to this Mystery" (*Diary*, 141). The two voices together, the one never giving the other any peace. Doubt as the condition of faith, not its opposite, making faith possible as (the) im/possible. When he wakes in the morning there is an overwhelming sense of meaninglessness, of nothing, making it hard to put his feet on the floor. Still, a beautiful sunrise that morning draws him beyond himself and the constraints of his life in the neighborhood. There is nothing to do but to go on, to follow the killing routine, whatever it all means. The Big Church at least supplies him with the opportunity to be there, to live "with

and for people here as much as I am able" (*Diary*, 157). That will
have to do. He is not a theorist and he offers no social vision. With
Dorothy Day, he thinks the soup kitchen and hospitality are the
real work, and the real church is the work. A social vision is less
important than the corporal works of mercy (*Diary*, 190). There
is no payoff—"You do it because you are here and the thing needs
doing" (*Diary*, 193). He is not trying to amass spiritual capital to
cash in on judgment day.

He is an anachronism, a medieval man, a celibate priest, "trying to use obsolete norms to make my way" (*Diary*, 201). He is an
obsolete man with a classical training, a love of Gregorian chant,
and a love of the contemplative life, who reads John of the Cross,
Simone Weil, the two Theresas—big (Avila) and little (Lisieux)—
and the biographies of Catholic saints. "All this makes me feel
like an anachronism, a museum piece, a curiosity, someone stuck
in an outworn medieval mind set" (*Diary*, 213), a monk trying to
practice an asphalt spirituality. His austere but serene suburban
seminary just across City Line Avenue equipped him to do valiant
battle—in the thirteenth century, which is a million miles away,
not in North Philadelphia, which is less than ten miles away, or
in a world menaced by nuclear weapons (*Diary*, 212). Celibacy
is also impossible, self-destructive, warping one's human sensi-
bilities, imposing a lethal solitude, discouraging vocations, and
yet also a condition of his service, making possible a dedication
not otherwise available; the difference between spending oneself
unconditionally for an intimate circle of wife and children, or for
everyone. McNamee is sophisticated, literate, well read, another
in a long line of gifted Irish poets and priest/poets—but for him
the academic life always constituted a temptation (*Diary*, 209). He
does not want to be an academic priest, just a priest, a real priest
in the working church, like Damian, who lived among the lepers
and was eventually contaminated. But of course he cannot really
be Damian either. When things get difficult, his suburban friends
take him to a good restaurant for a much-needed break; or they pay
for a trip to Donegal; or they give him a used, but by neighborhood
standards luxurious, car. Besides, his pantry is always full. So he is
always out of place. This is where he belongs, but he doesn't belong
here. His life is impossible, *the* impossible. There is "not much we
can do in the end but follow the Gospel. 'Give to everyone who
asks of you' [Luke 6:30]" (*Diary*, 239). Except, one cannot quite do

that either. You have to draw a line somewhere, and sometimes, for sanity's sake, not answer the phone or the doorbell.

This is a diary of "this mystery we call God," instead of a direct naming of God—an indirection he borrows from Karl Rahner (*Diary*, 88)—from which the "step/not beyond" is not far away. God is the Lord of this Joycean chaosmos. The text is filled with a faith in the unfathomable mystery of God, who is Lord both of the cosmos and of this chaos, a confession of faith that borders at times on a confession of absurdity. God is mysterious love, but this whole world is so loveless and wildly cruel that this is not to be believed. This world is mad with cruelty, and yet the news from Bangladesh this morning is accompanied by the beauty of an azalea in full bloom outside the rectory (*Diary*, 73). Unrelieved suffering in the neighborhood, but at this very moment down at "the shore," the Atlantic coast an hour or so drive away, the seagulls swing gracefully overhead, the sun rises over the ocean on a brilliant morning. We must believe and we cannot believe that love holds everything in the palm of its hands. Both together. The unspeakable, unintelligible cruelty of existence along with some pulsating event of love and mercy revealed in the little Irish sister, say, who quietly serves the wretched of the earth and does not get any headlines. What must be believed cannot be believed—that is the mystery we call God.

The work McNamee describes belongs to an ancient and radical element in Christianity. Richard Holloway puts it perfectly:

> Few of the followers of Jesus in history have been able to maintain the kind of uncompromising compassion that is celebrated in the Sermon on the Mount. The Church itself, which began as an outsider group in the Roman Empire, was soon seduced by the attractions of power and, wherever it established itself, learnt how to collude with it to its own worldly benefit. But there has always been a radical element in Christianity that has remained courageously loyal to the vision of Jesus. You find these radical disciples everywhere—in African shanty towns and South American barrios, American ghettoes and British sump housing estates—identifying themselves cheerfully with the dispossessed, and courageously challenging the systems that oppress them. Poor in spirit and in heart, they keep alive the challenge of Jesus to the thoughtless excesses of the powers that rule the world, proving that the Sermon on the Mount is still one of the most subversive utterances in history. [2]

While McNamee might challenge the bit about "cheerfully," Holloway describes exactly what I mean by the uncontainable "event" that Christianity contains, a radically deconstructive event, an event of *the* impossible. McNamee has gotten there by reading the prophets, the Gospels, the saints, and Daniel Berrigan, not Jacques Derrida, in whom he shows no interest.[3] Still, on my accounting, if deconstruction means the affirmation of the impossible, then deconstruction hits the ground here under the name of God—it being understood that this affirmation can be made under many names, with or without God. The gospel is not a set of doctrines but a way of life, what McNamee calls the *working* church, the one where truth means *facere veritatem*, making the truth happen. If the New Testament is a "theory," Kierkegaard said, then it is absurd, and the way not to be scandalized and repelled by the absurdity is what Kierkegaard called "faith," which takes the leap and translates the gospel into existence. Where love is implemented, there is the church. *Ubi caritas, ibi ecclesia.* Those who love—the text makes no special mention of Catholics—are born of God (1 John 4:7). Anyone, period! Where it is not translated into blood and prayers and tears, into "works of love," no amount of theology, candles, vestments, incense, or polished black hearses can make up the difference (more Kierkegaard).

The official Church, the one with the hierarchy, the seminaries, the buildings, the power, and the theology, would love to have a chance to close St. Malachy's, all the St. Malachy's (if it could be spared the bad publicity). Nothing would make more sense. Why? Why would the Church close this church? Why would the Church turn on the kingdom of God? "No money. No Catholics." There may be a better example than the Church of something that contains an event that it cannot contain, of trying to prevent the event by which it is constituted—but at the moment I cannot think of one! It makes perfect administrative sense to close these churches where there are no Catholics, where there are mostly poor black (non-Catholic) children otherwise destined for drugs, destitution, and despair, and to redirect resources to serve the parishes where there are well-heeled Catholics who need the sacraments and where there are prospective vocations. What could make more managerial sense than that? What could be more cost effective? The Catholic Church is not in this for its health! There is no free lunch. The Church has to be about its own business (not the Father's!). Would it not be mad to do otherwise? Of course. No argument. But it happens that such madness is called the foolishness of the cross, the holy madness of the kingdom of God. Read the New Testament. For that matter, read the papal encyclicals!

This is a diary of the gift, of a life of unconditional service, without payoff or guaranteed return. McNamee is not in this for a reward; he is not looking to cash in the accumulated chips of sticking it out in North Philadelphia (without asking for a transfer to the suburbs) in exchange for a bigger share in the heavenly banquet. St. Malachy's is not a prudent long-term celestial investment for him. He does not deny that there is a heavenly banquet, but he tries not to dwell on that. That is not going to get him anywhere. This work has to be done, with or without heaven. Heaven, he says, is for another day, and there is no time to waste on thinking about heaven. "That promise does not figure large in my own prayer or work. It would seem a betrayal of my real task, which is to make life here a little easier" (*Diary*, 46). That is almost exactly what Derrida means by the gift: giving in a moment of madness, without the expectation of return, whether or not there is one, even if economies are inescapable. Life is a gift that one gives. McNamee is on a spiritual journey that looks a lot like the one we were describing in chapter 2, one without a very clear idea of where one is going or whether one is making progress, a journey in which, for the most part, one is constantly asked to go where one just cannot go!

The effective but unthematic workings of an auto-deconstructive event in the *Diary* explain why so many of the binary oppositions on which the wheels of the official Church turn are so artfully undermined in this text—or perhaps we should say where these wheels are "stolen," to stick to the scene of North Philadelphia.

Here we meet the unaborted children whom the Right deserts as soon as they are actually born—into families where the father is in jail (if the father is known), abandoned by their mother, and raised (if they are lucky) by a destitute grandmother, who cannot raise them. These children cut beneath the distinction between Catholics and non-Catholics, between who is inside and who is outside the church. They cry out to us with all the power of powerlessness, with all the power of the gospel—for such as these is the kingdom of God, Jesus said. What does it matter whether they are Catholics if they *are* the kingdom of God?

Notice, too, the radical hermeneutic of faith that emerges in this text and its interweaving of faith and doubt, beyond the distinctly Cartesian and modernist opposition of "certitude" and "doubt." The harshness of the world that crushes one's spirit on these streets makes it impossible to believe anything. At some deep point in his heart McNamee thinks such unbelief is the cold truth. What gentle spirit hovers over these killing fields? Nothing, nobody, *nada*, never was. Still, the impossibility of belief in something, somewhere, is equally impossible—belief as the impossibility of impossibility, believing because it is impossible that this impossible absurdity is final. McNamee has written a kind of contemporary urban *Confessions*, pouring out in a radically honest and heartfelt way the doubts that constitute the very stuff of his faith. Faith does not subsist in simple polar opposition to doubt but remains embedded in doubt all the way down; it coexists with doubt, which is why it is faith and not some kind of privileged access to a higher knowledge, as if a believer is somebody hardwired to God on high and authorized to speak on God's behalf. A faith insulated from doubt fuels fanaticism and high-handed triumphalism and is in love with itself and its own power. Such faith soundproofs the walls of the intramural boys club called "the Church," the big visible one on top with all the bureaucrats and vestments. Faith is faith, and not a sword with which to slay the enemies of God (usually a cover for describing one's own enemies!), if and only if it is haunted by an equally inescapable anxiety that perhaps our words and prayers are just so much cosmic noise that will soon enough dissipate into entropic emptiness, menaced by an uneasiness that perhaps our works of mercy are just the stirring of so much cosmic dust on the surface of a little ball in an obscure corner of the universe, soon to be forgotten.

The same auto-constructive forces make themselves felt in McNamee's hermeneutic of prayer, in which prayer is the one recourse that keeps him from complete breakdown, the one escape that saves him just before he goes under, like the hero of one of those cheap television melodramas he watches before going to bed in the hope of driving the nightmare of his day from his mind lest it revisit him in sleep. Except he is denied that escape and prayer too is impossible. Prayer is *the* impossible. On the one hand, the confident prayer of a community, the gorgeous tones of the monks of Solesmnes, or even the fiery blasts of a local Baptist church driven by a first-rate organ and choir full of powerful lungs, people who know to whom they are praying. On the other hand, a much more radical prayer to an unknown God, of praying with no sense or assurance that anyone is out there to hear his prayers, an arid, destitute desert "khoral" prayer, abandoned, leaden (*Diary*, 165), desolate, and deserted in a dark night of the soul with no sense whatsoever that anyone is there on the other end. Prayer is prayer when prayer is impossible; otherwise it is a convenience. *Eloi, Eloi, lama sabachthani* is a perfectly auto-deconstructing prayer: it is addressed to God—which presupposes our faith that we are not abandoned—and asks why God has abandoned us.

By the same token, the hollowness of official orthodoxy is exposed by the robust event of a radical hospitality. McNamee is as orthodox as they come. He is an ordained priest who is faithful to a vow of celibacy, says his rosaries, loves the saints, worships before the Monstrance (exposed Holy Eucharist), likes stained-glass windows, clings to the Mass and the Eucharist, is horrified by abortion, and never mentions having any historical-critical doubts about the authenticity of the narratives of the New Testament that sustain him daily. What separates McNamee from the hierarchy in the Chancellory Office downtown is not that they have the orthodox faith and he is heterodox but rather the radicalized evangelical *hospitality* he practices, or tries to practice, toward all those who knock on his door (which seems like everybody all the time). By the same token, the people doing the impossible in the streets, the grandmothers trying to raise the children, these are women who don't come to Mass on the Feast of the Assumption, which is a "holy day of obligation," who don't know it is the Assumption and may have never even heard of it. Yet that is where the kingdom of God is at work, not among the diocesan bureaucrats, with the latest in faxing technologies, busily processing annulments for white Catholics in the suburbs.

Furthermore, the women also have a way of turning the tables on the men in the *Diary*. The church is found in the sisters, the little Irish nun who works in the slums of Belfast, in the sisters that work in the school at St. Malachy's, while the men who hold the hierarchical power are parasites who live off the real church sustained by these women. The ordained men in the hierarchy are fraudulent; the unordained women are the real church. Has not God chosen to confound the power of the men who glory in their masculinity, in possessing the physical likeness of the masculine Jesus, by way of unordained women who are the authentic image of Jesus?

Of course, in a deconstructive analysis, a simple distinction between inauthenticity of the hierarchical Church and the authenticity of the working church must not be allowed to close over. The power of the one to bleed into the other cannot be excluded. Consider the courage of archbishops like Desmond Tutu in South Africa and Óscar Romero in El Salvador and the bishops and theologians of South America who were intent on leading the church in the direction of radical evangelical service of the peasants. Or the brilliant teachings of Cardinal Joseph Bernardin, whose doctrine of the seamless garment of nonviolence across the board is a light to the church. Or the social encyclicals of the popes that call for radical justice. Or—forever the progressive's hero—Pope John XXIII, who presided for five years over what now seems a veritable Vatican Camelot. All this belies a simple opposition between two polar opposite churches. Moreover, we cannot ignore the sad story of corruption in the working church. One need only think of "Covenant House," a famous Catholic shelter in New York City that was wracked by charges of the sexual abuse of children lodged against Fr. Bruce Ritter, who was forced to resign in disgrace. Just as sadly, in 2006, a posthumous charge of sexual abuse was made against Fr. David I. Hagan—the beloved "Father Dave"—one of McNamee's closest friends and a hero of the *Diary* who also appears in the David Morse film and was once portrayed by George Kennedy in a made-for-TV film.[4] The charges were made a year after Hagan died of kidney cancer. Hagan, a fellow priest who figures broadly in the *Diary*, ran a halfway house in North Philadelphia for homeless children and young men and was a grade-school basketball coach of Hank Gathers, the Loyola Marymount basketball superstar who collapsed on the court and died of a heart attack in 1990. Everyone who knew Fr. Dave was outraged by the charges, but the story hangs over his name like the smog that drifts over the dirty, dangerous streets of North Philadelphia, the lingering ambiguity an apt image of the ambiguity of life itself and the difficulty of making clean and safe distinctions.

Theo-Drama: Ikon's Postmodern Liturgy

I turn now to a second and interestingly different case study.
McNamee says he is a displaced medieval man who finds himself
walking the streets of North Philadelphia, and he makes no mention of "postmodernism." True enough; but I would argue that
while the high theory of deconstruction, the names of Derrida or
Foucault or "postmodernity," are nowhere to be found in his text,
its tropes and movements are everywhere at work. That contrasts
with my second case study, which is the work of a small grassroots
group in Belfast named Ikon: young men and women dedicated
to addressing peace and reconciliation issues in Northern Ireland,
whose "manifesto," as it were, *How (Not) to Speak of God*, was
recently published by its founder Peter Rollins.[5] Rollins is trained
and literate about postmodern and especially Derridean theory,
and he embraces the idea of a postmodern "emergent" church. So
the two cases converge and diverge in complementary ways.

Let me emphasize, for the sake of clarity, the change of scenery
in these two cases. For all its radicality, St. Malachy's is a parish in
the Archdiocese of Philadelphia and a traditional ministry, with a
rectory, a weekly schedule of masses and the sacraments, parish
committees, a parish school, a parish bulletin board, and all the
usual outer trappings of institutional life, with a Cardinal Archbishop overseeing the whole operation. "Ikon" is nothing of the
sort. It is an independent avant-garde assembly (but remember that
"assembly" is a perfectly good translation of the Greek *ecclesia*) of
young laypeople, intellectuals, church and community activists,
including non-Christians, who all meet in a bar. It has no buildings, assets, hierarchy, ordained ministers, seminaries, or bulletin
boards. These people are making it up as they go along, not out of
whole cloth, but out of the memory of Jesus and the promise of
the kingdom. St. Malachy's is an institution that struggles against
institutionality; Ikon is hardly an institution at all, a more literally
and visibly deconstructive quasi-institution. It is relatively new
and no one knows how long it will be around.

For all his radicality, McNamee is a deeply traditional man, an
ordained Catholic priest who tries to celebrate a traditional liturgy
in the debris of capitalism and late modernity. He is disheartened
by the low numbers of people who attend St. Malachy's, by the low
regard for the Mass and the Eucharist, and by the fact that he can-

not compete with the passion, impromptu, and improvisations of
the black Baptist churches in the neighborhood. Still he does the
best he can with a traditional liturgical service, and he works hard
to do it as well as he can, even if nobody shows up. Ikon is not a
parish but a decidedly postmodern paraliturgical undertaking, an
attempt to produce an avant-garde liturgy. No one is ordained, there
is no ethical or theological consensus, only a concerted effort to be
inclusive, both liberal and conservative, Catholic and Protestant,
theist and atheist. Its members meet in a Belfast bar and create
experimental liturgies or performances. Again, while McNamee
condemns a church preoccupied with sexuality even as Rome (so to
speak) is burning down all around it, he never addresses questions
of gay and lesbian rights, in or out of the church. Were he pursued
on this point I think he would strike a completely tolerant attitude,
while likely considering it the sort of problem that comes up only
if you are no longer drugged out, starving to death, or homeless.
For Ikon, however, homophobia is one of the questions that needs
to be addressed, and it does this in an interesting way.

St. Malachy's is a church, Ikon not quite. On the margins of
the church, far removed from the center of ecclesiastical power,
St. Malachy's is still an archdiocesan church. Ikon is not so much
a church as an experimental group in which an alternate church
and a paraliturgy are being reinvented in a postmodern mind set.
Or else Ikon is simply a working church without a Big Church,
a central authority, theology, or any buildings of its own, that is,
without a hierarchical church of which it is the subversive underbelly. Or else it is simply not church at all, not religion (*Speak
of God*, 44–46), but a kind of religion without religion, moving
out beyond the traditional borders of religion, in a way that Jesus
himself might be understood to have done, where the ministry
of service to the despised and outcast cuts across the borders of
Jew, Samaritan, and Roman centurion. To illustrate this point,
Rollins refers us to the Costa-Gavros film *Amen*, in which a Catholic priest living in the Third Reich proposes to his cardinal that
all Catholics convert to Judaism on the grounds that the Nazis
would not then dare to carry out the deportations against so large
and prominent a population. When the cardinal not surprisingly
declines the novel suggestion, the priest tearfully renounces his
beloved faith, becomes a Jew, and boards the train to Auschwitz
(*Speak of God*, 63).

As the title suggests, *How (Not) to Speak of God*—adapted from the title of a famous essay by Jacques Derrida on negative theology[6]—is written in a spirit of mystical modesty and religious unknowing. It proceeds from a strong sense of what McNamee, following Rahner, would call "the mystery that we call God," which elicits a multiplicity of interpretations, of ways/nonways to speak/ not speak of God. God is precisely the one of whom we cannot speak (adequately) and so cannot not speak, cannot stop speaking about. As Meister Eckhart said, God is unnameable and (there-fore) omninameable, and so Meister Eckhart prays, "I pray God to rid me of God."[7] I pray (the unnameable) God to rid me of (the idol I have named) God. Whence the figure of the "ikon": words that respect God's transcendent excess as opposed to the "idol" of thinking we have captured God with our limited words and concepts, a central distinction derived from the Catholic thinker Jean-Luc Marion, whose work pervades the book.[8] The postmod-ern God shatters our concepts of God—this in line with a very ancient tradition of negative theology. Idolatry comes in many forms. Literalizing the truth of the Scriptures is idolatrous in a way that parallels the idolatry of the church in Catholicism, of which McNamee complains throughout his text (without using that language). Orthodoxy is idolatry if it means holding the "cor-rect opinions about God"—"fundamentalism" is the most extreme and salient example of such idolatry—but not if it means holding faith in the right way, that is, not holding it at all but being held by God, in love and service. Theology is idolatry if it means what we say about God instead of letting ourselves be addressed by what God has to say to us (iconic). Faith is idolatrous if it is rigidly self-certain but not if it is softened in the waters of "doubt."

How (Not) to Speak of God offers an interesting and fertile foray into postmodern theory in the first half of the book, but it is its descriptions of an experimental liturgy in the second half, titled "Orthopraxis," that constitute a kind of applied postmodernism— postmodernism on the ground—that interest me here. The mem-bers of Ikon are not academics but activists. Ikon is a concrete, community-based, practical, and paraliturgical undertaking, less interested in theology than in "theo-drama." The second half of the book describes ten sample services, or experimental liturgies, of which I single out two, the first and the last, which model how to reinvent the church in the unforeseeable future.

The point of the first service, "Eloi, Eloi, Lama Sabachthani" (My God, My God, Why Have You Forsaken Me?), is to revisit Holy Saturday, when Jesus, having lamented his abandonment by God, lies dead and buried, the disciples are scattered, and no one knows anything about a resurrection. These events pose the question of imitating Jesus in radical terms, the figure of *kenosis* I described earlier, with no promise of a payoff. This is quite like McNamee's conviction that "there is no payoff," that one takes care of business in the street because one is there and it needs to be done, even if one is done in by so doing. One does what one must do, outside an economy of exchange.

The scene is the Menagerie Bar in Belfast, lit by a hundred candles. As a disc jockey plays music while occasionally chanting "Eloi, Eloi, Lama Sabachthani," a woman writes the English translation on a canvas set on a nearby easel, and a projector casts the image of Hans Holbein's "The Body of the Dead Christ in the Tomb" on a space on the wall. A young man takes a microphone at the foot of the bar's stage and tells the story of a community founded by followers of Jesus who, dispirited after the crucifixion, went off thousands of miles from Jerusalem to live their lives guided solely by the teachings of Jesus, while knowing nothing of his resurrection. After three hundred years of isolation they are discovered by Christian missionaries, who tell them of the resurrection and ascension. On hearing this news, the elder of the group is anguished. While conceding this is cause for celebration, the elder is also worried. Up to now, he says, we have "forsaken our very lives for him because we judge him wholly worthy of the sacrifice, wholly worthy of our being" (*Speak of God*, 80), knowing that the death that defeated Jesus will likewise overtake them, not because it promised a long-term payoff. Then the speaker asks why they struggled to be like Jesus, which offers us another variation on our question: *why* do what Jesus would do?

A new speaker goes up to one of two tables on the stage and leads a Good Friday service of "Tenebrae" (darkness), during which the church is lit only by candles (as is the bar), all but one of which is gradually extinguished, signifying hope in the promise of the resurrection. Then a second speaker tells of a dream set in a cathedral in which a weeping woman dressed in black lays flowers at the foot of the crucifix and then crosses over to the side of the cathedral and extinguishes all the candles and closes the

Bible on the altar. God is dead, the divine word silenced—and the woman is Mary. The drama concludes with these two interpretations: a single candle of light and hope versus all light and hope extinguished. We are not asked to choose one. (As Derrida would say about a situation of undecidability, we live in the distance between the two.) The final scene of the theo-drama takes place on judgment day, in which it turns out the devil is the gatekeeper of eternal happiness and he asks us to choose between eternal life, if we would but acknowledge him as Lord, or else eternal death with Jesus. This is not the end of faith, the speaker says, but the moment in which faith is forged and our motives purified. It is also a scene described in classic spirituality when the saints tell us that (*per impossibile*) they would rather spend eternity in hell for the love of God than in heaven if that violated God's love, which is essentially what Derrida means by the gift.

The tenth and final theo-drama is titled "Queer," which is not, as you might expect, a simple affirmation of gay and lesbian rights in the church but something slightly different. As the bar fills up, a bare-chested young man stands motionless on the bar stage while a woman writes on his body "gay," "queer," "homosexual," "faggot," and "sodomite" while rocks lie strewn around the two figures. A speaker addresses the gathering and says that Ikon is neither a liberal nor a conservative Christian voice, because both those voices have to do with questions of orthodoxy, holding the right view, whether that be Left or Right. Rather, Ikon is a place in which people care for one another in Christ. "During this sacred hour" we check our Left/Right orthodoxies at the door of the Menagerie. Here there is no gay issue, only mutual love and support. Ikon is for straight and gay, for liberal and conservative, for those who believe in God and those who do not. One needs to take a view on this divisive issue, no doubt, but not here, the very sacredness of this space being defined by suspending all "stands" and making everyone welcome at the table in virtue of their Christlikeness. Another speaker explains that the stones on the stage represent our judgments, our stands (or what Derrida would call "positions," as distinguished from the deeper "affirmation" that underlies "positions"), which we are all too ready to hurl at one another.

The drama makes plain that suspension of judgment is the very essence of the "sacred space." That is why a Belfast bar can be a sacred space while an imposing cathedral might be anything but. To be sure, the matter of gay and lesbian rights must be settled as best it can—and I for one have taken a "stand" or a "position"—but not here, not in this place. Presumably, when a stand is taken, it will not take the form of a stone. I am reminded by this service from Ikon of Jean-Yves Lacoste's view of "liturgy" as being constituted by a certain *epoche*, in which the forces that drive the "world" (winning, payoffs, economies) are suspended so that the liturgical hour may be an hour of eschatological peace. The liturgical hour is not the actual eschaton, which is to come, but a quasi-eschatological performance, a dramatic presentation or enactment of the eschaton, in which we live *as if* for one hour the age of eschatological peace had arrived. In that sense, there is nothing parasitic or "paraliturgical" at all about Ikon—this is the very heart of liturgy.[9]

Conclusion: After Deconstruction

Jesus, I have argued, is the centerpiece of a "poetics" of the "kingdom of God" found in the New Testament, of a kind of theo-poetics—not of a politics or an ethics or a "church dogmatics"—in which the task of converting that poetics into reality falls squarely on our shoulders. It is up to us to implement it, to make it come true, in the spirit of what Augustine and Derrida call truth as *facere veritatem*, doing or making the truth. So I am always on the look out for ways to make that happen, to make or let the kingdom come, to make the event come true. It is in that spirit that I have introduced these two books, which are not intended simply as more scholarly stuff to hold library shelves firmly in place, not intended to generate still more books (like this one!), nor are their authors coming up for tenure or promotion. They mean to bear witness to a working church. Read them like the message at the beginning of *Mission Impossible* (just so!), which self-destructs as soon as it is read in order to get us down to the business of the mission itself, which is indeed nothing less than *the* impossible. The two cases are quite different from each other but they complement each other nicely. Each one in its own way translates into an institutional setting what I have been saying about deconstruction and the theo-poetics of the kingdom. Each is a marginal community, outside the mainstream corridors of power, laboring among or on behalf of what Paul called *ta me onta*, the nothings and nobodies of the world. You are not well-born, not well heeled, Paul tells the Corinthians rather bluntly, and woe to you if you are, Jesus adds! The spirit of Jesus, his poetics of the kingdom, is not counted among the forces of the "world" but rather is counted amid the remnants, ruins, and debris of the world, where he himself lived and died. That is the tension that is structurally built into the "institutional" church.

In the *Diary*, a traditional church retaining a conventional form has to struggle on the margins of the Big Church, barely surviving on its edge. Life is lived here on the brink—of financial extinction (its parishioners have no money), of the physical and mental exhaustion of McNamee and his staff trying to make this impossible thing happen, of the sheer extinction of the people who live in mayhem, where life is just so destitute and dangerous that one fears it simply won't survive at all. In Ikon, a nonconventional and experimental church, an alternative church, tries to reinvent the tradition, to reimagine classical theology, to rethink God and Christ and church, not so much on the level of doctrine or dogmatics but as a practice, a performance, indeed as a certain experimental theo-drama, a parasitical, postmodern liturgy.

These two cases describe what a church might look like *after deconstruction*, not after it is over but after the manner of deconstruction, after its point has been absorbed, when we understand what deconstruction is after, what it is up to. When something is deconstructed, it is not razed but reconfigured and transformed in response to inner and uncontainable impulses. When something is deconstructed, it takes on a certain look, not unlike the look of these two communities, among other unforeseeable and un-programmable possibilities. On this point, deconstruction differs from Kierkegaard's "attack upon Christendom." I am deeply fond of Kierkegaard and of the lampooning that he gave the Danish clergy in the last two years of his life—"God's men" as he called them with consummate irony, meaning that they were entirely, down to the toes hidden by their long robes, the world's men, who earn a profitable living off the crucifixion. But I have come to conclude that, much as I love him, Kierkegaard was over the top in those final years, in part because of the utterly cynical view he finally took of sexuality and marriage, which said a great deal more about his own pathology than about Christianity, but also because it is hard to imagine what any possible institutional church would look like after Kierkegaard. He said he was offering a "correction" to the church, but it is harder to see what a church with a Kierkegaardian correction would be and easier to think there just would be no church.[10]

But nothing of the sort can be said of deconstruction. Once, when he was accepting an honorary degree from the New School of Social Research in New York City, Derrida used the occasion to try to dispel the misunderstanding that deconstruction is *against* institutions, when all along it is a philosophy *of* and *for* institutions, a way to keep institutions alive and well and on the move.[11] In that sense deconstruction is a deeply "conservative"[12] force, where fidelity to an institution requires a certain infidelity, while rigid fidelity to rules and regulations spells *rigor mortis* for the corporate body. (He added that he is especially for institutions that grant him honorary degrees.) A glance at his biography will reveal a lifelong commitment to founding innovative and experimental institutions that push against the limits of institutional conventionality. Institutions tend to become the enemy of the very event they are supposed to embody, intent on preserving their own existence, even at the cost of the very purpose of their existence. They are, as Derrida said, prone to practices of "auto-immunity," to immunize themselves against themselves.[13] The Bush administration's treatment of the US Constitution is a good example: we have to suppress our democratic love of the principle of due process, of the rule of law, and the separation of powers in order to win the battle against terrorism. We must be willing to suppress what the United States stands for as an idea and an ideal in order to serve and preserve our national interests. The United States first, then the principles of democracy later, if there is time and opportunity. The sexual scandal besetting the Catholic Church in America is another good example. First the sexual molestation of children entrusted to its care, then the institutional cover-up, which means the institution immunizing itself against what it stands for—"for it is to such as these that the kingdom of God belongs" (Mark 10:14). Indeed, the figure of Jesus in the New Testament is still another example of a deconstruction of a religious world portrayed as putting conditional cultic observances before what those observances were supposed to be about—the unconditional love of God and neighbor.

Thus an institution modeled *after* deconstruction would be auto-deconstructive, self-correcting, removed as far as possible from the power games and rigid inflexibility of institutional life, where a minimal institutional architecture pushes to some optimal point, near but not all the way to anarchy, some point of creative "chaosmos."[14] The institutional ideal in this case is to do the impossible, to make the impossible happen—as far as possible. Such an anarchical an-architecture is good advice for the church; indeed, it is a very ancient instruction and of venerable origin:

> You know that among the Gentiles those whom they recognize as their rulers lord it over them, and their great ones are tyrants over them. But it is not so among you; but whoever wishes to become great among you must be your servant, and whoever wishes to be first among you must be slave of all. For the Son of Man came not to be served but to serve, and to give his life a ransom for many. (Mark 10:42–45)

That is a kind of managerial madness that is the very foolishness of the kingdom of God, which Jesus demonstrated in his own life. Jesus was an outspoken critic of the powers that be, which cost him dearly. To implement the kingdom of God, to translate this poetics into praxis, into a working institution, requires affirmation and reaffirmation, imagination and reimagination, a willingness to go ahead in impossible situations, a willingness to reinvent itself in an ongoing self-renewal of itself. The church, charged with the realization of the kingdom, requires a repetition with a difference, lest it freeze over into infidelity to itself and immunize itself against itself, suppressing the very event of the kingdom of God that is its mission, its mission impossible, to express.

The good news deconstruction bears to the church is to provide the hermeneutics of the kingdom of God. The deconstruction of Christianity is not an attack on the church but a critique of the idols to which it is vulnerable—the literalism and authoritarianism, the sexism and racism, the militarism and imperialism, and the love of unrestrained capitalism with which the church in its various forms has today and for too long been entangled, any one of which is toxic to the kingdom of God. The deconstruction of Christianity is nothing new. It is the ageless task imposed on the church and its way to the future, the way to be faithful to its once and future task, to express the uncontainable event from which the church is forged. To engage the gears of deconstructive thought and practice is not to reduce our beliefs and practices to ruins, which is the popular distortion, but to entrust oneself to the uncontainable event they contain, breaking down their resistance to their own inner tendencies and aspirations, exposing them to the call by which they have been called into being, which here, in the case of the church, is the kingdom that we call for, the kingdom that calls on us.

But what, then, is the kingdom of God? Where is it found? It is found every time an offense is forgiven, every time a stranger is made welcome, every time an enemy is embraced, every time the least among us is lifted up, every time the law is made to serve justice, every time a prophetic voice is raised against injustice, every time the law and the prophets are summed up by love.

From time to time the figure of Jesus, or fragments of his figure, appear here or there in individual lives, showing up sometimes in people who burn with a prophetic passion, sometimes in people of inordinate compassion and forgiveness. When this happens, we are likely to mistake such people as mad or weak, which in a sense they are—mad with the folly of the cross, weak with the weakness of God.

Notes

Foreword

1. People without Doctorates.

Chapter 1 *In His Steps*—A Postmodern Edition

1. Charles Sheldon, *In His Steps: What Would Jesus Do?* (New York: Grosset & Dunlop, n.d.). All references to this work appear in the text and are to this edition, which advertises itself as "The Complete Authorized Edition" and "Complete and Unabridged." It has a foreword by Sheldon dated 1935. This is the oldest edition I have seen and my thanks to Sharon Baker at Messiah College for giving it to me. *In His Steps* is available online at: www.ssnet.org/bsc/ihs/ihs.html.

2. Actually, nineteenth-century Kansas, the home of John Brown, was a progressive state, as opposed to present-day Kansas, whose school boards are still struggling to come to grips with Darwin!

3. For what follows on Sheldon, see James H. Smylie, "Sheldon's *In His Steps*: Conscience and Discipleship," *Theology Today* 32 (April 1975): 32–45, who summarizes the book and the debate and defends Sheldon against various critics. See also Chris Armstrong, "Holiness of Heart, Life, and Pen: Charles Wesley and Charles H. Sheldon," *Christianity Today*, www.ctlibrary.com/ch/2005/issue85/11.43 .html; and Armstrong, "How Would Jesus Pastor?" www.christianitytoday.com/ le/2007/001/7.43.html. For a critique of Sheldon, see Paul S. Boyer, "*In His Steps*: A Reappraisal," *American Quarterly* 23, no. 1 (Spring 1971): 60–78.

4. John Howard Yoder, *The Politics of Jesus*, 2nd ed. (Grand Rapids: Eerdmans, 1994), 4n7.

5. "When you are about to meet someone, especially someone who seems to be distinguished, put to yourself the question 'What would Socrates or Zeno have done in these circumstances?' and you will not be at a loss as to how to deal with the occasion" (*The Enchiridion or Manual of Epictetus* 33, available at www.ptypes .com/enchiridion.html). My thanks to Bruce Benson of Wheaton College for drawing my attention to this quote.

6. Visit www.calltorenewal.org/.

7. Mark C. Taylor, *Erring: A Postmodern A/theology* (Chicago: University of Chicago Press, 1984), 6. The first book on Derrida and theology in English was Carl Raschke, *The Alchemy of the Word* (Missoula, MT: Scholars Press, 1979), revised and reissued as *The End of Theology* (Denver: Davies Group, 2005).

8. No wonder that in March 2005, Senate Commerce Committee Chairman Ted Stevens (R-Alaska) told the National Association of Broadcasters that he would push for stricter broadcast "decency" standards in cable television and subscription satellite TV and radio.

The Right understands well the potential of such art and does not want the ugly underbelly of American capitalism so graphically exposed. The Right is offended by the saucy language, but their tender natures are not offended by the indecency of capital punishment or by the pornography of a war without cause or justification. Fortunately, the midterm elections of 2006 relieved Mr. Stevens of his chairmanship.

9. Johannes Baptist Metz, *Faith in History and Society* (New York: Seabury, 1980), 88–118.

10. Deconstruction can wear many hats and travel under many names. Calling it the "hermeneutics of the kingdom of God" is what happens when it sets up shop in biblical religion.

11. The masterwork of the great New Testament scholar Edward Schillebeeckx was a lengthy two-volume work titled, respectively, *Jesus* and *Christ*. The joke used to circulate that a third volume was forthcoming to be titled *Superstar*. In my variation on that quip, the third volume would have been titled *Deconstructor.*

12. Dostoyevsky's cardinal scolds Jesus for having laid an intolerable burden of freedom on humankind. Wanting human beings to love God freely, Jesus was willing to sacrifice their most basic needs, but the church has corrected that. The vast majority of humankind does not need risk but security; they do not want freedom but bread. The three temptations of Jesus by the devil are three great missed opportunities. Jesus failed to see that it was only if the church could feed the hungry that it could expect virtue from sinful humankind. In failing to hurl himself from the roof of the temple to prove that he was the Son of God, Jesus overestimated the capacity of weak men to believe without miracles to sustain their faith. The church has satisfied the needs of the body for bread and of the conscience for certainty and replaced the torment of ambiguity and free choice with "miracle, mystery, and authority," and these wretched, weak creatures were happy to make the exchange. When the cardinal finished, Jesus, who had been silent the entire time, simply approached the old priest and kissed him. Then the cardinal, disarmed by the kiss, opened the door and commanded Jesus to leave, never to return. A great story, but not perfect. Feeding the hungry and healing the heart were conjoined parts of Jesus's ministry—he came teaching *and* healing, the both together (Matt. 4:23–25). Furthermore, I do not think Jesus held the exaggerated proto-existentialist idea of radical freedom attributed to him by Dostoyevsky but insisted instead that we be like the lilies of the field and put our trust in God.

13. James K. A. Smith, *Who's Afraid of Postmodernism? Taking Derrida, Lyotard, and Foucault to Church*, The Church and Postmodern Culture (Grand Rapids: Baker Academic, 2006).

14. I fleshed out the scholarly details of this claim in *The Prayers and Tears of Jacques Derrida: Religion without Religion* (Bloomington: Indiana University Press, 1997).

15. See John D. Caputo, *The Weakness of God: A Theology of the Event* (Bloomington: Indiana University Press, 2006), 101–24.

16. See Alfred Loisy, *The Birth of the Christian Religion*, trans. L. P. Jacks (New Hyde Park, NY: University Books, 1962), 295; online at www.earlychristianwritings.com/loisy/chapter9.html.

17. Since I first wrote this chapter, Anne Lamott's *Plan B: Further Thoughts on Faith* (New York: Penguin, 2005) was brought to my attention by James Smith. Lamott has written a felicitous story of postmodern faith that turns on the same figure of speech and has the spirit of saucy uncertainty that makes up faith that I heartily recommend.

Chapter 2 Spiritual Journeys, Postmodern Paths

1. Charles Sheldon, *In His Steps: What Would Jesus Do?* (New York: Grosset & Dunlop, n.d.), 18–19.

2. Jacques Derrida, *Of Grammatology*, corrected edition, trans. Gayatri Spivak (Baltimore: Johns Hopkins University Press, 1997), 158. For a sober account of what Derrida means by this, see James K. A. Smith, *Jacques Derrida: Live Theory* (New York: Continuum, 2005), 43–45.

3. Bobby Kennedy often used the variations of this quotation, which Teddy Kennedy also cited in the eulogy he gave at Bobby's funeral; the quotation actually originates with George Bernard Shaw.

4. If "religion" is a Latin, Western word, then in order to engage in a genuine confrontation with cultures other than our own it is not enough to engage in "comparative religion," which is to cast the question in our own terms, as are attempts to compare Western ideas of God with other ideas. That leads to the ineptness of Pope John Paul II's declaration that Buddhists are "atheists."

5. See Edmund Husserl, *Cartesian Meditations*, trans. Dorion Cairns (The Hague: Martinus Nijhof, 1960), §54, which every reader of continental philosophy should commit to heart.

6. There is a perfectly simple historical explanation of the ambiguity, which arose from using the substantive *pas* to reinforce a negation, as in, *Je n'avance pas*, which literally means, "I do not move forward, not even a step." On this account, *pas* as "not" (*ne*) is simply shorthand for "(not a) step" (*Littré*, "Pas.2").

7. There are always historical or contextual reasons for this. For example, the word "outgoing" can mean "retiring," as in "the outgoing president," or the very opposite of "retiring," as in "the one sister is quite outgoing, but the other is retiring."

8. Martin Heidegger, *Off the Beaten Track*, trans. Julian Young and Kenneth Haynes (Cambridge: Cambridge University Press, 2002); Maurice Blanchot, *The Step Not Beyond*, trans. Lycette Nelson (Albany: State University of New York Press, 1992).

9. *Republic* 6.509b.

10. The three "theological" virtues differ from the four "cardinal" virtues of practical wisdom, justice, courage, and temperance first identified by Plato and Aristotle. A cardinal virtue—from the Latin *cardo*, meaning "hinge"—is a stable foundation of human conduct that turns on the Greek ideals of reason and moderation, of avoiding excess or defect. Too much courage is foolishness and too little is cowardice. But the theological virtues are marked by the excess of love, which is why there is a thin line between faith and fanaticism, a line we should never deny. If the cardinal

virtues are hinges, the theological virtues are for the (lovingly) unhinged! See John D. Caputo, "The Axiology of the Impossible," in *The Experience of God: A Postmodern Response*, ed. Kevin Hart and Barbara E. Wall (New York: Fordham University Press, 2005), 20–41.

11. Jacques Derrida, *The Post Card: From Socrates to Freud and Beyond*, trans. Alan Bass (Chicago: University of Chicago Press, 1987).

12. Bart D. Ehrman, *Misquoting Jesus: The Story behind Who Changed the Bible and Why* (New York: Harper Collins, 2005).

13. And all this by way of a commentary on Edgar Allan Poe's "The Purloined Letter"! Derrida was mainly offering a commentary on psychoanalysis. The psychiatrist does not just "retrace the steps" of the patient's symptoms and lead him or her back to the hidden trauma, like a detective tracking down clues, but brings the patient around to recognizing the trauma. There is *no way* to make the "step" back to the trauma; there is just a "not," the recognition of that dead end or impasse supplying what healing there is.

14. "God" is like that: the very conditions under which we understand what God means—infinity, say—make it impossible for us to understand what God means. Anselm said that by God we mean that than which no greater can be conceived, which means that in order to characterize God, Anselm had to come up with an "auto-deconstructing" concept: the concept of something that cannot be conceived, the concept of something that exceeds any possible concept.

15. A comparable analysis can be made of the religious idea of being "created," where to be created is to be called into being, which in turn means, when you think about it, to answer a call we never heard. This is the beautiful way it is put by Emmanuel Levinas.

16. Derrida elaborates the chance analogies between them—they are both North Africans (Algiers/Ancient Numidia), teary sons of protective mothers, who sneak away to the Big Apple (Paris/Rome), Derrida being born on the *rue Saint Augustin*, etc.—in "Circumfession: Fifty-nine Periods and Periphrases," in Geoffrey Bennington and Jacques Derrida, *Jacques Derrida* (Chicago: University of Chicago Press, 1993). He is even a slightly "atheistic" Augustine, by the standards of the local pastor or rabbi (see *Jacques Derrida*, 155), but more deeply considered he is interestingly "religious." For commentaries, see my *The Prayers and Tears of Jacques Derrida: Religion without Religion* (Bloomington: Indiana University Press, 1997), 281–307; and *Augustine and Postmodernism: Confessions and Circumfession*, ed. John D. Caputo and Michael Scanlon (Bloomington: Indiana University Press, 2005).

17. Catherine Malabou and Jacques Derrida, *Counterpath: Traveling with Jacques Derrida* (Stanford, CA: Stanford University Press, 2004).

18. "Circumfession" (p. 1) turns on a similar experiment, a bet that Geoffrey Bennington writing (on the top half of the page) a commentary "on" Derrida (down below) will not anticipate everything Derrida will have said.

19. See Augustine, *Confessions* 8.12.

20. What Derrida imbibed by being born and raised in an (assimilated) Jewish family, he relearned on a different level later from Levinas, who gave it a stunning (if difficult) Greco-philosophical formulation. The Jewishness of Levinas and Derrida is an important part of the link with (the Jewishness of) Jesus.

21. Catherine Keller, *The Face of the Deep: A Theology of Becoming* (New York: Routledge, 2003), 12–13, 87, 169–70.

22. In *Being and Time*, trans. John Macquarie and Edward Robinson (New York: Harper & Row, 1962), §62, Heidegger says that an "authentic" human life is marked by a "resolution" that must not become "rigid" but "held open"; we retain the freedom to take it back, amend it, or even reverse it. When St. Paul picked himself up, dusted himself off, and got back on that horse, he was not any less resolute than before but he was ready to reconsider where he had been going. One may be all along resolved but the specifics of the resolution may shift, even quite dramatically.

Chapter 3 A Prayer for the Impossible

1. I am also making use here of the sense of "event" in Gilles Deleuze, *The Logic of Sense*, trans. Mark Lester with Charles Stivale, ed. Constantin V. Boundas (New York: Columbia University Press, 1969).

2. Jacques Derrida, *Politics of Friendship*, trans. George Collins (New York: Verso, 1997), 1–25.

3. Johannes Baptist Metz, *Faith in History and Society*, trans. David Smith (New York: Seabury, 1980), 88–99.

4. Deleuze, *Logic of Sense*, 149.

5. Walter Benjamin, "The Concept of History," 9, in *Walter Benjamin: Selected Writings, 1938–40*, vol. 4, ed. Michael Jennings (Cambridge, MA: Harvard University Press, 2003), 389–400.

6. Jacques Derrida, "As If It Were Possible, 'Within Such Limits' . . ." in *Negotiations: Interventions and Interviews: 1971–2001*, trans. Elizabeth Rottenberg (Stanford, CA: Stanford University Press, 2002), 343–70.

7. Jacques Derrida, "Afterw.rds or, at least, less than a letter about a letter less," www.hydra.umn.edu/derrida/after2.html; "*Sauf le nom* (Post-Scriptum)," trans. John Leavey Jr., in *On the Name*, ed. Thomas Dutoit (Stanford, CA: Stanford University Press, 1995), 43.

8. See Mark Dooley's interview of Jacques Derrida, "The Becoming Possible of the Impossible," in *A Passion for the Impossible: John D. Caputo in Focus*, ed. Mark Dooley (Albany: State University of New York Press, 2003), 21–33, where Derrida uses this phrase as a marker for God. It also goes a long way toward marking off what we in the West mean by "religion," i.e., as a certain covenant with the impossible, a point I explore in depth in *The Prayers and Tears of Jacques Derrida: Religion without Religion* (Bloomington: Indiana University Press, 1997).

9. Jacques Derrida, "The Force of Law: 'The Mystical Foundation of Authority,'" trans. Mary Quantaince, in *Deconstruction and the Possibility of Justice*, ed. Drucilla Cornell et al. (New York: Routledge, 1992), 3–69. All references to this essay appear in the text. I strongly recommend the first half of this essay, pp. 3–29, as one of the best ways into deconstruction that I know; the second half is a difficult interpretation of a strange essay by Walter Benjamin.

10. For purposes of economy I am omitting Derrida's earlier work, which only seems to look less friendly to theology. That omission is unforgivable, which on Derridean grounds invites your forgiveness. Let me say this much here and then beseech the reader who really cares to read further, especially *Of Grammatology*, corrected edition, trans. Gayatri Spivak (Baltimore: Johns Hopkins University Press, 1997), at least through p. 164. Derrida follows Ferdinand de Saussure's revolutionary notion of structural linguistics. Saussure pruned the study of language of the

classical and ornate terms of "ideas" in the "soul" (metaphysics) or in "consciousness" (psychology) that are "expressed" in "words" and correspond to "reality" and
proposed a simpler, more streamlined and scientific approach. Think of Saussure
(a Genevan) as being like John Calvin and John Knox in sixteenth-century Geneva
coming up with a leaner, meaner version of Christianity! He used a scientific and
functional model of "signifiers" as "arbitrary" (it does not matter whether you
say *roi* or "king") and "differential" (just so long as we can discern the difference
between *roi* and *loi* or "king" and "sing"), which work in virtue of the "space" (or
differential) between them. A language is a coded string of signifiers constituted
by their differences from one another, a point that can be seen intuitively by con-
sulting a dictionary, in which words are defined by other words. A "speaker" is
not some interior thinking thing who outwardly "expresses" already constituted
"ideas" but a place where particular linguistic utterances (*parole*) called "events"
occur—that is one of the sources of this word in French philosophy—in virtue
of the rules of the linguistic system (*langue*). Personal consciousness is displaced
and preceded by an impersonal differential system or "structure." Saussure, like
Marx and Freud, thought it is an illusion to consider people as pure autonomous
agents, which is criticized as "humanism," by which he did not mean "acting hu-
manely." Think of "humanism" as a kind of "linguistic Pelagianism," the heresy
of thinking too much of pure human autonomy and not recognizing that human
beings come into the world always already marked—not by inherited sin but by
inherited social, linguistic, and historical systems or structures.

Derrida criticized Saussure on two points: (1) The privileging of speech over
writing. While we learn to speak before we learn to write, on the strictly scientific
terms set by Saussure, that is merely a psychological, not a structural, point. The one
no less than the other is a form of arbitrary differential "spacing," without regard to
whether it occurs in a written or a spoken medium. Speech is just a way of writing
with air, an instance of "archi-writing" (or *différance*). (2) The "structure" (*langue*)
is not a closed system but an open one. There is not a finite set of rules (*langue*)
that precontains in principle every possible sentence that any given speaker could
ever come up with (*parole*) that anticipates every possible "event." For example,
no one can set an a priori limit to the metaphors that can be constructed or to
the chance "events" that occur in puns, creative misuse, misunderstanding, etc.
Think of James Joyce or the Internet, which "disseminates" in a way that is very
close to what Derrida means by linguistic "dissemination." Language is a system,
not a Hegelian or "totalizing" system, but an open-ended one, like the World Wide
Web. "Deconstruction" does not "destroy" something but loosens it up, opening
it up to invention, novelty, and innovation, not absolute novelty, but the novelty
that comes from innovating on the existing system. When Derrida emphasized the
"unprogrammable"—and "undecidable," a word borrowed from mathematician
Kurt Gödel that has been scandalously misrepresented—he meant this innovative
open endedness of the system.

Derrida summarized these two innovations under the neologism *"différance"*—
spelled with an "a"—a graphic (written) misspelling that in French is phonically
undetectable (i.e., a homonym). In coining this word, Derrida was (1) indicating
that language is constituted by spacing or differences; (2) contesting the privilege of speech and marking its graphic (or differential) character; (3) pointing
how signifiers stand in for and so "defer" the presence of things; and (4) trying

to perform in the concrete the inventiveness of language whose theory he was defending. *Différance* is a word that exhibits what words do, which is impossible, because if *différance* caught on, as it did, it would just become one more word in the language, not a word for what language does. So "différance" was an early example of *the* impossible.

Because of these criticisms of Saussure, Derrida is better described as a "post-structuralist," a term that has been drowned out by "postmodernism," which has a looser cultural significance going back to architecture. Derrida rejects both terms and embraces the "modern" Enlightenment project of social and political emancipation. Unlike Lyotard, he has no objection to a "metanarrative of emancipation" and advocates a New Enlightenment free of the illusions of the old one. Derrida went beyond his early interest in language—as well as in the phenomenology of Husserl, which would also need to be analyzed—to form a wider philosophical point of view. The criticism of the priority of speech over writing is ripe with social, political, and theological import—like the war between Judaism and Christianity. "The Jews" are people of the dead letter, of the written contract, legalists, an eye for an eye, a tooth for a tooth; but the Christians live with the breath of the spirit, by the word of honor, by love and the gift (see Shakespeare's *The Merchant of Venice*). The privilege of speech over writing is part of a more basic system as old as Western culture itself: life over death, soul over body, spirit over matter, eternity over time, man over woman, original over copy, human over animal, being over becoming, etc.

Such hierarchies constitute what Derrida famously condensed into the phrase the "metaphysics of presence," a binary system privileging "presence" over "absence" (*Of Grammatology*, 49). On this schema, men are full presence and women are defined as missing something. Against this, Derrida argued, first, that the superior member of a binary pair is subverted by its inferior member, the way speech turns out to be a form of "writing" (with air) or the "master" both depends on and becomes dependent on the "slave" in Hegel. That is what Derrida called "reversal." But second, both members of the pair are variations on a third that is prior to each (the movement of "displacement"). For example, neither speech nor writing should be privileged since both are a form of differential spacing (= *différance*) prior to both. Or again, in the New Testament, first a strategic reversal privileges the poor and warns woe to the rich, then displacement occurs because we are all children of God. Moreover, "ethical difference" has been a central part of the lexicon of deconstruction ever since 1964, when Derrida took up Levinas's "ethics of the other," belying the too simple schema of an "early" Derrida concerned with literature and a "later" Derrida concerned with ethics and politics. Derrida is not undermining all distinctions but showing that distinctions are better thought of differentially, as occupying different points along a continuous line, where elements of one thing blend and bleed into others, and demonstrating that the "black-and-white," either/or way of thinking in terms of binary oppositions—where one thing is simply the lack of the other—is invidious and loaded with traps. We cannot understand men or women if we do not first understand what is womanly about men and manly about women (reversal); both "man" and "woman" are traps that prevent the invention of new forms of gendered existence that shatter traditional stereotypes (displacement). That gives a church with a long history of patriarchy—not to mention unresolved tensions between "Christian and Jew" or "Christian and Muslim"—something to think about. For a start on all this, see *Deconstruction in a Nutshell: A Conversation with Jacques Derrida*, edited with a commentary by John D. Caputo (New York: Fordham University Press, 1997), and James K. A. Smith, *Jacques Derrida: Live Theory* (New York: Continuum, 2005).

11. Theodore W. Jennings Jr., *Reading Derrida/Thinking Paul* (Stanford, CA: Stanford University Press, 2006).

12. See Richard Kearney, "Deconstruction and the Other," in *Debates in Continental Philosophy: Richard Kearney in Conversation with Contemporary Thinkers* (New York: Fordham University Press, 2004), 139–56. Kearney conducts a brilliant interview with Derrida, which is a superb place to start the reading of Derrida's work.

13. Jacques Derrida, *The Gift of Death*, trans. David Wills (Chicago: University of Chicago Press, 1995), chaps. 3–4.

14. The following discussion of the gift is based on Jacques Derrida, *Given Time, I: Counterfeit Money*, trans. Peggy Kamuf (Chicago: University of Chicago Press, 1991), chap. 1; see esp. pp. 6–7, 9–10, 30–31.

15. See the interesting exchange between Marion and Derrida in *God, the Gift, and Postmodernism*, ed. John D. Caputo and Michael J. Scanlon (Bloomington: Indiana University Press, 1999), 42–47, 54–78.

16. The sort of gift Derrida has in mind happens to teachers who influence students they no longer remember, by having said things they do not remember saying.

17. See Jacques Derrida, *Cosmopolitanism and Forgiveness*, trans. Mark Dooley and Michael Hughes (New York: Routledge, 1997).

18. For a good example of evangelical madness, see HBO's 2007 film *Longford*. It is a marvelous presentation of the true story of a deeply Christian man, Frank Pakenham, the seventh earl of Longford, whose belief in forgiveness ruined his public career when he took up the cause of child-killer Myra Hindley. Jim Broadbent is a superb Longford.

19. See E. P. Sanders, *Jesus and Judaism* (Philadelphia: Fortress, 1985) for a superb account of Jesus's position on forgiving sin, which I am following here.

20. Jacques Derrida, "Hostipitality," in *Acts of Religion*, ed. Gil Anidjar (New York: Routledge, 2002), 362.

21. Ibid.

22. Richard Kearney, Jacques Derrida, and I debated this point in *God, the Gift, and Postmodernism*, 130–36.

23. Kierkegaard is especially protective of the paradox here: do not try to write this off as an "act of charity" with charity-house food. The Scriptures are explicit: this is a "banquet" and everything is the best. See *Kierkegaard's Writings*, vol. 16, *Works of Love*, trans. and ed. Howard Hong and Edna Hong (Princeton, NJ: Princeton University Press, 1995), 81–84.

24. Jacques Derrida, *Points . . . Interviews, 1974–1994*, ed. Elisabeth Weber, trans. Peggy Kamuf et al. (Stanford, CA: Stanford University Press, 1995), 83.

25. Jacques Derrida, "Hospitality, Justice, and Responsibility," in *Questioning Ethics: Contemporary Debates in Philosophy*, ed. Richard Kearney and Mark Dooley (New York: Routledge, 1999), 77–79.

26. Ibid.

27. *"Les non dupes errent," Séminaire oral du 14 Mai 1974, Seminaries de Jacques Lacan: 1973–74,* available online at http://perso.orange.fr/espace.freud/topos/psycha/psysem/nondup/nondup13.htm.

28. Emmanuel Levinas, *Ethics and Infinity,* trans. Richard Cohen (Pittsburgh: Duquesne University Press, 1985), 67.

29. Derrida, *On the Name,* 74.

Chapter 4 Jesus, the Theo-Poetics of the Kingdom, and Praxis

1. See John D. Caputo, "Beyond Sovereignty: Many Nations under the Weakness of God," *Soundings: An Interdisciplinary Journal* 89, nos.1–2 (Spring-Summer 2006): 21–35, from which the previous two paragraphs are borrowed.

2. *Meister Eckhart: The Essential Sermons, Commentaries, Treatises, and Defense,* ed. Bernard McGinn and Edmund Colledge, Classics of Western Spirituality (New York: Paulist Press, 1981), 183–84.

3. I elaborate on "theo-poetics" as a "sacred anarchy" in the second half of *The Weakness of God: A Theology of the Event* (Bloomington: Indiana University Press, 2006); for a sketch of it, see esp. pp. 13–17.

4. See Jacques Derrida, *Rogues: Two Essays on Reason,* trans. Pascale-Anne Brault and Michael Naas (Stanford, CA: Stanford University Press, 2005), and note 1 of chap. 4 above.

5. See John D. Caputo and Catherine Keller, "Theopoetic/Theopolitic," *Cross-Currents* 56, no. 4 (Winter 2007): 105–11, from which the previous four paragraphs are borrowed.

Chapter 5 What Would Jesus Deconstruct?

1. Susan Pace Hamill, *The Least of These: Fair Taxes and the Moral Duty of Christians* (Birmingham, AL: Sweetwater, 2003). For references to the debate spawned by this book and for a full bibliography and description of Hamill's work, visit www.law.ua.edu/directory/view.php?user=40.

2. See Lisa San Pascual, "The Social Gospel Lays an Egg in Alabama," *Religion in the News* 6, no. 3 (Fall 2003): www.trincoll.edu/depts/csrpl/RINVol6No3/Social%20gospel%20lays%20egg.htm; Jim Wallis, *God's Politics: Why the Right Gets It Wrong and the Left Doesn't Get It* (New York: Harper Collins, 2005), 243–45; Bob Riley, "It's Time to Choose," www.governorpress.state.al.us/pr/sp-2003–05–19-session.asp.

3. Wallis, *God's Politics,* 368.

4. Tony Campolo maintains that there are 2,000 verses of Scripture that call us to respond to the needs of the poor (www.answers.com/topic/tony-campolo).

5. The Christian Coalition of Alabama also opposed Amendment Two—which would have written that right into the state constitution—on the grounds that it may eventually cost them money, clearly the sort of thing that always worried Jesus; see www.ccbama.org/emailalerts/ea011805.asp.

6. Ronald Sider, *The Scandal of the Evangelical Conscience: Why Are Christians Living Just Like the Rest of the World?* (Grand Rapids: Baker Books, 2005); and Sider, *Rich Christians in an Age of Hunger: Moving from Affluence to Generosity* (Nashville: Word, 2005). In addition, a recent study shows that if you exclude Warren Buffet, in 2006 the "Slate 60" (sixty richest billionaires) made charitable

148   Notes to Pages 94–96

contributions of $7 billion, out of an estimated $630 billion in assets—about 1 percent ("Why Do the Richest People Rarely Intend to Give It All Away?" *New York Times*, March 1, 2007, C3).

7. Jacques Derrida, *Given Time, I: Counterfeit Money*, trans. Peggy Kamuf (Chicago: University of Chicago Press, 1991), 2n2. One can no doubt hold such a view about private charity in good faith but one should be given pause by how agreeable this is to the corporations and the wealthy who bitterly opposed such legislation.

8. Dale Martin, *Sex and the Single Savior: Gender and Sexuality in Biblical Interpretation* (Louisville: Westminster John Knox, 2006); see Martin's "Introduction" on "textual agency." Texts do not "do" anything; we do things with texts.

9. John D. Caputo, *The Weakness of God: A Theology of the Event* (Bloomington: Indiana University Press, 2006), 101–24.

10. Richard Holloway, *How to Read the Bible* (London: Granta, 2006), 86.

11. Garry Wills has returned to this point in *What Jesus Meant* (Baltimore: Penguin, 2006) to insist that Jesus is neither a Democrat nor a Republican; rather, he insists on the difference between politics and an otherworldly kingdom.

12. See, for example, Vernard Eller, *Christian Anarchy* (Eugene, OR: Wipf & Stock, 1999).

13. You might express your deep concern for the poor by warning that rushing to the aid of the weak and defenseless will make them even weaker and more defenseless. The place where Jesus expresses this concern may be in another lost manuscript but, never fear, I have found a supplementary source—the social Darwinists and Nietzscheans, whose sales may henceforth soar in Christian bookstores. I agree with Simone Weil, who said that to engage in charitable works without humiliating the recipients who really need help is as hard as walking on water. That is the paradoxical logic of the gift: as Derrida said, be on the alert to all the twists and turns the gift may take, but then give! But we may be forgiven for wondering why the Right is not equally worried about the disabling effects of wealth, about unproductive lives of pure consumption, especially about living idly off inherited fortunes. When Warren Buffet gave away most of his fortune, he said he left enough for his children to be able to do anything, but not enough to do nothing. It was precisely such accumulating inequalities that the "year of the Jubilee" was meant to level. So if we build good schools in the worst neighborhoods, with well-paid teachers, the latest equipment, comprehensive facilities—just like the white children have—and if we offer meals for children too hungry to concentrate on their studies and day-care support for working parents, that will surely ruin and enfeeble those little children! You will forgive me if I seem cynical; it is, I have to concede, an innovative reading of the Sermon on the Mount.

14. Garry Wills, "Christ among the Partisans," *New York Times*, April 9, 2006, 12.

15. Thanks to Rev. Thomas Martin OSA, director of the Augustinian Institute at Villanova University, for the quip and the information. The text is not found in the Augustinian corpus.

16. We can be grateful for astonishing expressions of private charity—Bill and Melinda Gates, Warren Buffet, Oprah Winfrey—without ignoring the veritable laissez-faire market economy that has allowed such excessive fortunes to accumulate. Peter Singer has recently examined what a fair-share contribution to the

public good is in "What Should a Billionaire Give and What Should You?" *New York Sunday Times*, December 17, 2006. Lou Dobbs, not exactly a Marxist, details the attack on the middle class in *War on the Middle Class: How the Government, Big Business, and Special Interest Groups Are Waging War on the American Dream and How to Fight Back* (New York: Viking, 2006). In a capitalist system such as ours we not only need private means but public ones as well. In the Hurricane Katrina disaster the scale of the destruction overtook local resources and required the swift intervention of the federal government, which failed, in my view, because it was administered by people who do not think that governments are there to help the poor. Capitalism is a heartless system that, left to its own dynamics, crushes the weakest elements. There is nothing Jesus-like about it. If it can produce wealth, as it can, it also requires regulation.

17. Families flourish best in the middle; nothing is more destructive of "family values" than the extremes of wealth and poverty generated by the forces with which the Christian Right has gotten in bed.

18. To learn more about this, visit the Sojourners/Call to Renewal website: www.sojo.net and www.calltorenewal.org/. For a comparable prophetic Jewish voice in contemporary politics, see the work of Rabbi Michael Lerner at www.tikkun.org/.

19. For a good presentation of the sense and range of the encyclicals, see Judith Merkle, *From the Heart of the Church: The Catholic Social Tradition* (Collegeville, MN: Liturgical Press, 2004).

20. Jacques Maritain, *Integral Humanism, Freedom in the Modern World, and A Letter on Independence*, rev. ed. (Notre Dame, IN: University of Notre Dame, 1996).

21. Lieutenant General William Boykin, a deputy secretary of Defense in the Bush administration, said, "Why is this man in the White House? The majority of Americans did not vote for him. He's in the White House because God put him there for a time such as this" (www.telegraph.co.uk/news/main.jhtml?xml=/news/2003/10/17/wboyk17.xml).

22. Luke 22:35–38 might be used as a cover for self-defense, but I am inclined to see it is as setting the stage for Luke 22:49–51; it is certainly the only suggestion to the contrary of the many sayings on nonviolence and is unattested by Mark or Matthew.

23. The passage about "hating" one's father and mother is illustrated in Sheldon's *In His Steps* when those who follow Rev. Maxwell in working in the ghettos of "Tennesseetown" do so at the cost of angering and alienating their loved ones. Jesus is talking about doing what is right even if it makes your family miserable, not recommending that we bear anyone ill will. See also chap. 5 n. 31, below.

24. See Daniel Maguire, *The Moral Core of Judaism and Christianity* (Minneapolis: Augsburg Fortress, 1993). Maguire shows the diversity of Catholic opinion on abortion, birth control, and same-sex marriage ("Bishops Denounce Writings of Catholic Theologian," *New York Times*, March 23, 2007, A15) and that a Catholic could treat legalized abortion as a lesser evil, following Augustine (*De ordine* 2.4) and Aquinas (*Summa Theologica* II-II, Q. 11, a. 10), who also tolerate legalized prostitution as a lesser evil (*New York Times*, June 29, 2007, Letters to the Editor).

25. For a critique, see John B. Cobb, Richard A. Falk, Catherine Keller, and David Ray Griffin, *The American Empire and the Commonwealth of God: A Political, Economic, Religious Statement* (Louisville: Westminster John Knox, 2006).

26. See the various statements of the US Conference of Catholic Bishops on a wide range of social justice issues, including the war in Iraq, at www.usccb.org/bishops/iraq.shtml.

27. See Jacques Derrida, *Archive Fever*, trans. Eric Prenowitz (Chicago: University of Chicago Press, 1995).

28. Alain Badiou, *Saint Paul: The Foundation of Universalism*, trans. Ray Brassier (Stanford, CA: Stanford University Press, 2003) has sparked widespread interest in St. Paul among contemporary philosophers, such as Georgio Agamben and Slavoj Žižek.

29. See Luce Irigaray, "Equal to Whom?" in *The Essential Difference*, ed. Naomi Schor and Elizabeth Weed (Bloomington: Indiana University Press, 1994), which is a review of Elizabeth Schüssler Fiorenza, *In Memory of Her: A Feminist Theological Reconstruction of Christian Origins*, 2nd ed. (New York: Crossroad, 1994).

30. In addition to *In Memory of Her* (New York: Crossroads, 1983), which is a classic, see also Schüssler Fiorenza's *But She Said: Feminist Practices of Biblical Interpretation* (Boston: Beacon, 1992). On this point I applaud the courageous act of "canonical disobedience" in the recent ordinations of women priests; see Rose Marie Berger, "Rocking the Boat: A New Wave of Catholic Women Answers the Call to Ordination Priesthood—An Act of Ecclesial Disobedience," *Sojourners*, March 2007, www.sojo.net/index.cfm?action=magazine.article&issue=soj0703&article=070322.

31. Two other points here that deserve further discussion: (1) Of the dwindling numbers of men attracted to the Catholic priesthood, where mandatory celibacy is compounded by the exclusion of women, one can only say that one reaps what one sows. There is an ancient tradition, both Christian and non-Christian, of voluntary celibacy as a religious discipline to train the mind and heart on God alone. (Of course, raising several children well is an equally demanding discipline.) Celibacy is a venerable spiritual practice, and it can play a crucial role for men and women dedicated to radical social justice, who can live and work among the poor in a way that is not practical for people with families and children. All power to it—but not all coercion. (2) It is amusing to compare the Christian Right on "family values" with the sorts of things said about families in the New Testament. Jesus seems to have shocked his family and the locals in Nazareth, who did not know what to make of him, and he himself said that you had to be prepared to hate your father and mother if you wanted to follow the way, and that his word would divide father from son, daughter from mother, and bring enemies into the house (Matt. 10:35). Jesus was on a mission, whatever his family thought. It does not sound like "Ozzie and Harriet."

32. Visit www.guttmacher.org/pubs/fb_induced_abortion.html.

33. Visit www.informationclearinghouse.info/article11674.htm.

34. *State of the World's Children*, 1st ed. (UNICEF, 2005); the statistics on HIV/AIDS are from a joint UNAIDS and WHO report found at www.who.int/hiv/mediacentre/2006_EpiUpdate_en.pdf.

35. On Paul and homosexuality, see E. P. Sanders, *Paul* (Oxford: Oxford University Press, 1991), 110–13. For especially insightful recent work, see Martin, *Sex and the Single Savior*, and Mark Jordan, *The Invention of Sodomy in Christian Theology* (Chicago: University of Chicago Press, 1997).

36. Martin, *Sex and the Single Savior*, "Introduction."

37. The hypocrisy of the Religious Right on this issue is regrettable. While studies show that more than half of HIV/AIDS cases are caused by blood transfusions, drug use, or heterosexual activity, the Christian Right does not hesitate to perpetuate the falsehood that AIDS is a biblical condemnation of homosexual love. That is the sort of hypocrisy that Jesus vigorously denounced, and one can imagine him today flaunting his association with the victims of AIDS against the long robes of the Christian Right, just like those New Testament scenes in which he healed the lepers and associated himself with his own society's untouchables in defiance of the temple authorities. See John Gallagher and Chris Bull, "Perfect Enemies: The Religious Right, the Gay Movement, and the Politics of the 1990s," *The Washington Post* (1996) at www.washingtonpost.com/wp-srv/style/longterm/books/chap1/perfectenemies.htm. On the causes of AIDS/HIV, see the NIH report "The Evidence that HIV Causes AIDS" at www.niaid.nih.gov/factsheets/evidhiv.htm.

38. If someone objects that I cite Schüssler Fiorenza and Johannes Baptist Metz a lot—two people who do not do "deconstruction" but "critical theory"—I reply that on this point as on so many others the divergence between the two was grossly exaggerated, which was confirmed in the final years of Derrida's life by the reconciliation of Derrida and Habermas. See *The Derrida-Habermas Reader*, ed. Lasse Thomassen (Chicago: University of Chicago Press, 2006). For a more deconstructively flavored blend of theology, politics, and feminism, see the works of Catherine Keller and Ellen Armour.

39. Hans-Georg Gadamer, *Truth and Method*, 2nd rev. ed., trans. Joel Weinstein and Donald Marshall (New York: Continuum, 2005), 310.

40. Elizabeth Schüssler Fiorenza, *Bread Not Stone: The Challenge of Feminist Biblical Interpretation* (Boston: Beacon, 1986), ix–xvii, 10–15, 39–41.

41. Augustine, *De doctrina Christiana* 1.36.40.

42. The hermeneutical imperative under which the church stands is not a straightforward proportion (a to b) but a proportionality (a:b :: c:d): to meditate on how Jesus responded to the requirements of his times and then invent a way to do likewise in ours.

43. Based on Exod. 21:22–23, to kill a pregnant woman is murder, payable by a life for a life, but to injure her and cause a miscarriage is not and merits only a fine. The earliest Jewish tradition gives precedence to the life of the mother and treated the fetus as a person only when the head appears at birth. See Daniel Schiff, *Abortion in Judaism* (Cambridge: Cambridge University Press, 2002), available online at www.questia.com/PM.qst?a=o&docId=105535719. Had Jesus anything new to say on this subject, had he disagreed with any of this, that seems like the sort of thing that would have stood out and been recorded. We do know that he was concerned with the situation in which divorce would leave a woman in his day, which suggests that a pregnancy resulting from rape or incest, or one that puts the life of the mother in peril, poses circumstances to which Jesus would have been sensitive. We also know that he was opposed to inflexible rules.

44. Apart from the fact that Jesus and Socrates head up the list of the most famous innocent victims of capital punishment, consider its self-contradictory legal status: physicians, the most qualified people to administer lethal drugs without botching the job, are prevented by law from participating on the grounds that they have taken an oath to do no harm! For a recent report, see "The Death Penalty:

'Tinkering' to Good Effect," *America: The National Catholic Weekly*, February 19, 2007, 5.

45. Joseph Cardinal Bernardin, "A Consistent Ethic of Life: Continuing the Dialogue" (The William Wade Lecture Series, St. Louis University, St. Louis, MO, March 11, 1984). This lecture is available online at www.priestsforlife.org/magis terium/bernardinwade.html.

46. James Trussel, director of Office of Population Research, Princeton University, maintains that just under half of unwanted pregnancies are terminated. Based on that, proper use of emergency contraception pills alone, he maintains, could prevent some 1.7 million unwanted pregnancies annually and therefore something like 800,000 abortions. See Frank Davidoff, MD, and James Trussell, PhD, "Plan B and the Politics of Doubt," *Journal of the American Medical Association* 296 (2006):1775–78; online at jama.ama-assn.org/cgi/content/full/296/14/1775?ijkey=qsS31RMdFZfdU&keytype=ref&siteid=amajnls.

47. Louis Dupré, *Contraception and Catholics* (Baltimore: Helicon, 1964) is still a little classic that thoroughly routs the arguments against contraception.

48. I acknowledge the work of groups like "Samaritan's Purse" in Africa, but they are criticized for tying medicine too closely to the gospel, thereby supplying the Bush administration with an opportunity to link government programs to groups that discourage the use of condoms. Christians should be calling for the more massive relief that is possible only with a shift in federal budget priorities.

49. In *Politics* 7.16.1335b20–30, Aristotle permitted abortion for couples who "have children in excess," but limited it to the period "before sense and life have begun," which he marked at forty days for males and eighty to ninety days for females (*Natural History* 7.3). For Thomas Aquinas the fetus, while certainly a nutrient, sentient life before that point, had not yet attained the status of an identifiably human life ("delayed hominization"). For Augustine and Aquinas, abortion before then is not murder—not all killing is murder—but it is still a moral evil. See St. Augustine, *On Exodus* 21.80. See Thomas Aquinas, *Summa Contra Gentiles* 2.89; *Summa Theologica* 2, Second Part, Q. 64a.8, ad 2.

50. See John D. Caputo, *Against Ethics* (Bloomington: Indiana University Press, 1993).

51. While many Christian leaders have actually convinced themselves that homosexuals pose a bigger threat than global warming, there are encouraging signs of change. See the "conversion" in 2002 of the Rev. Richard Cizik, director of the National Association of Evangelicals, and a growing new movement grouped around the Evangelical Climate Initiative at www.christiansandclimate .org/statement.

Chapter 6 The Working Church

1. John P. McNamee, *Diary of a City Priest* (Kansas City, MO: Sheed and Ward, 1993). References appear in parentheses in the text.

2. Richard Holloway, *How to Read the Bible* (London: Granta, 2006), 88–89. Holloway has produced an incisive and amazingly compact thumbnail sketch of the Christian and Jewish Scriptures, and of Jesus in particular, that I highly recommend.

3. We need social theory and political theology, and we need to address structural issues that spawn all the North Philadelphias of this world.

4. For a newspaper report of the charges in the *Philadelphia Daily News*, June 17, 2006, see www.rickross.com/reference/clergy/clergy486.html.

5. Peter Rollins, *How (Not) to Speak of God* (Orleans, MA: Paraclete, 2006). References appear in parentheses in the text.

6. Jacques Derrida, "How to Avoid Speaking: Denials," in *Derrida and Negative Theology*, ed. Harold Coward and Toby Foshay (Albany: State University of New York Press, 1992), 73–142. In French, the title *"Comment ne pas parler: Dénegations"* might mean: how not to speak, how to not speak, how to not speak by speaking, how to speak in "denial," etc.

7. *Meister Eckhart: The Essential Sermons, Commentaries, Treatises, and Defense*, ed. Bernard McGinn and Edmund Colledge, Classics of Western Spirituality (New York: Paulist Press, 1981), 199–203.

8. Jean-Luc Marion, *God without Being: Hors-Texte*, trans. Thomas Carlson (Chicago: University of Chicago Press, 1991), 7–107.

9. Jean-Yves Lacoste, *Experience and the Absolute: Disputed Questions on the Humanity of Man*, trans. Mark Raftery-Skehan (New York: Fordham University Press, 2004), chap. 4.

10. See my interpretation of Kierkegaard in John D. Caputo, *How to Read Kierkegaard* (London: Granta, 2006), esp. chap. 10.

11. I have sketched out Derrida's attitude to institutions in *Deconstruction in a Nutshell: A Conversation with Jacques Derrida*, edited with a commentary (New York: Fordham University Press, 1997), chap. 1.

12. Derrida describes himself as "a very conservative person" (*Deconstruction in a Nutshell*, 8); for a gloss on this remark, see pp. 77–82 of that work.

13. Jacques Derrida, *Rogues: Two Essays on Reason*, trans. Pascale-Anne Brault and Michael Naas (Stanford, CA: Stanford University Press, 2005), 28–41.

14. Derrida himself was instrumental in establishing alternative institutions, like the College Internationale de Philosophie, whose purpose was to discuss topics that could not be found in standard university curricula, designing radically innovative courses in terms of content and employing experimental methods. There is no tenure for the professors at the College, no grades for the students, and all decisions are made in common, one person one vote, senior professors, first year students, and staff. For his main writings on institutions, see Jacques Derrida, *Who's Afraid of Philosophy: Right to Philosophy 1*, trans. Jan Plug (Stanford, CA: Stanford University Press, 2002); and *Eyes of the University: Right to Philosophy 2*, trans. Jan Plug et al. (Stanford, CA: Stanford University Press, 2004).

Index